Trail Guide Handbook

Cuyahoga Valley

National Recreation Area

The Cuyahoga Valley Trails Council, Inc.

with Photographs by Robert Muller

This publication is made possible through a generous grant from The George Gund Foundation, Cleveland, Ohio.

Published by the Cuyahoga Valley Trails Council, Inc., in cooperation with the Cuyahoga Valley Association.

Graphic design and initial layout by Glyphix, Kent State University.

Final layout and imagesetting: Enterprise Information Services, Akron, Ohio.

Cuyahoga Valley Trails Council, Inc., (CVTC) is a not-for-profit, all-volunteer organization dedicated to building and maintaining trails in the Cuyahoga Valley. CVTC was formed in 1985 from the Ad Hoc Trails Committee of the Cuyahoga Valley National Recreation Area Citizens Advisory Commission. Purposes of CVTC include promoting the implementation of the Cuyahoga Valley National Recreation Area *Trail Plan*, encouraging stewardship of trails and promoting preservation and conservation of natural areas through public education. CVTC publishes trail brochures and other educational materials, circulates a quarterly newsletter, *The Cuyahoga Valley Explorer*, and conducts monthly volunteer trail work projects. For more information, write: Cuyahoga Valley Trails Council, Inc., 1607 Delia Ave., Akron, OH 44320-1617.

The Cuyahoga Valley Association (CVA) is a not-for-profit organization which supports and promotes Cuyahoga Valley National Recreation Area. Founding members of CVA were among those supporting the formation of the national recreation area in the 1960s and '70s. In the succeeding years, CVA has aided the park's development by raising financial and volunteer support for CVNRA, co-sponsoring cultural arts events, including the annual Cuyahoga Valley Festival, and publishing educational materials. To join CVA, write: Cuyahoga Valley Association, P.O. Box 222, Peninsula, OH 44264.

Cover Photo: Pinery Narrows from Route 82 Bridge by Robert Muller. Background map courtesy of U.S. Geological Survey.

ISBN 0-9630416-0-6

Library of Congress Catalog Card Number: 92-114089

There are some who find a trailhead,
or a path through the woods which
curves invitingly out of sight,
simply irresistible.

Charles Little, Greenways for America

CONTENTS

FOREWORD

A Brief History of Trails in the Cuyahoga Valley

The earliest trail builders in our valley were the buffalo (bison) who had a natural knack for the best trail locations including fording places in the streams. The Indians adapted these trails, followed by the early settlers. Many of these trails played an important part in the early history of our nation—as shown on the ancient maps of early North America.

By 1923 when our small band of adventurers sought to "re-explore" the hidden places in the valley, these trails were long ago taken over by the area roadways, or grown over by the natural vegetation. Our small group of art students, garbed in the toughest clothing and shoes available in those popular "Army & Navy" stores of WWI vintage, ventured forth into this tanglewood of dense brush and trees—with barbed wire-like vines and poison ivy—formidable enough to make even Brer Rabbit look twice before entering! Our slogan was from the line in Kipling's poem, "The Explorer," which went something like this: "Something hidden—go and find it—Lost and waiting for you—Go!" and go we did, paying a dear price for the sweat-stained pages in our sketch books!

By the mid-1930s, some trail work was done in the valley, but only within the various parks existing then. This didn't help us much, and we had only the vegetation-choked towpath which ran through the full length of the valley. This trail work was done by the various work relief agencies—the W.P.A. and C.C.C. The latter did much trail work in the Kendall Ledges area.

It wasn't until Cuyahoga Valley National Recreation Area was established that trail work was begun within the valley proper. (How we could have used such trails years ago!) By the year 1991, there were many types of trails within the valley. Ski trails, short trails, long trails, trails to fit all shoe sizes, and even boardwalk trails where needed. Trail building had progressed much from our own early days. They no longer just "grew like Topsy" and ran helter-skelter over the hills and valleys. They are carefully planned now, by park architect and engineer, and carefully built by park crews, aided by groups of volunteer trail builders. (Their combined efforts and results deserve our heartiest thanks!)

The trails described in these pages, remember, are merely "paper trails." To get the feel and heft of the real trails, you should walk them, savoring each new view along them, ever-changing views, changing from day to day and season to season. Go and find for yourself that "something hidden" which Kipling spoke of!

Joe Jesensky
Akron, Ohio
July 1991

ACKNOWLEDGEMENTS

Can a committee write a book? After working with the "Big Guide" committee for over a year, we are convinced that this guide could not have been produced any other way! Each volunteer brought to the project his or her unique talent and personal familiarity with the trails of the Cuyahoga Valley. There is no way that all these talents could be found in one person alone. Their unabashed love of the valley and never-failing humor imbued the project with a joy and spirit that kept us persevering through all the deadlines and details.

The project began with an idea, several years ago, about the time that the Cuyahoga Valley Trails Council began producing individual trail guides for Cuyahoga Valley National Recreation Area. Why not print a guide to ALL the trails in the valley? Everyone thought it was a great idea-but who would do it? Then, thanks to the CVNRA staff, we learned that Dave Gates had been thinking about just such a guide. We put out a call for others interested and all of a sudden we had a small— but able— committee to begin what affectionately became known as "The Big Guide". The initial committee included: Peg Bobel, Rob Bobel, Tom Fritsch, Dave Gates, Jack Wenrick, and Jerry Welch.

Next, we needed field scouts to go out, hike or ride the trails, and report back with draft write-ups, and later to return to the field, drafts in hand, to check them for accuracy. We are grateful for the many hours spent hiking the beloved trails of the Cuyahoga Valley (somebody had to do it) by these scouters and writers: Carl Bochmann, Tom Fritsch, Jan Geho, Dick and Yvette Hoffman, Glen and Tom Jenkins, Barb and Mike Kaplan, Kathleen Pettingill, Chuck Urbancic, Annette Wasinski, Vera Riccardi, Dana Smith, Jack Wenrick, Jerry Welch, Aaron Wester, and Gene Wimmer.

While the scouters were out in the woods, the mappers set about putting lines on paper. Initial drafts were drawn up over a series of hot summer evenings by Rob Bobel, Jerry Welch, and Jack Wenrick , with final maps penned by Rob Bobel and Tom Fritsch. Kim Mueller volunteered to produce the excellent trailhead map. We are grateful to Dave Gates, who did the map photo-reduction and pasteup, and a special thanks goes to Jack Wenrick for generating the wording for the maps, and for acting as courier and making countless runs to keep the mapping moving!

Most of the writing, editing (and typing!) was done by Peg Bobel. Additional writing was prepared by Rob Bobel, Tom Fritsch, Dave Gates, Jan Geho, Jim Sprague, and Donna Studniarz. Rob Muller, who did all the photography, spent many a Sunday looking for that perfect shot that "tells the story". We think you'll agree he did. When we thought who would we most want to write a forward-all agreed that no one would be more appropriate than Joe Jesensky. Thanks also go to our final proofreader, Karen Parsons.

For official review, helpful suggestions, and support of the project, we gratefully thank the staffs of Cuyahoga Valley National Recreation Area, Cleveland Metroparks, and Metro Parks, Serving Summit County.

All this could not be accomplished without funding. We thank Tom Jenkins and the Cuyahoga Valley Association for preparing a funding request, and are most grateful to the George Gund Foundation of Cleveland, Ohio, for awarding us a grant to publish the guide.

The chores of working on this project were always overshadowed by the pleasures of working with the people who made this guide happen. We can not forget to thank the families and friends of the volunteers who assisted or were patient with our obsessions. They were in fact our inspiration.

Rob and Peg Bobel

INTRODUCTION

Learn of the green world what can be thy place. Ezra Pound

Newcomers to northeast Ohio are often surprised to find a green spot on the map between Akron and Cleveland. The curious discover that green spot to be the Cuyahoga River valley. Exploring the river valley, they are soon forced to give up the "steel mills and cornfields" impression of Ohio. What may come as a surprise to you as well are the cliffs and hemlocks that look like they belong in Canada, the clear, rippling streams coming from forested hills that look like smaller versions of the Appalachians and Alleghenies, and the farmsteads and villages suspended in time.

Much of this green valley is now known as Cuyahoga Valley National Recreation Area (CVNRA), a unit of the National Park System. Of the Cuyahoga River's entire length, one-fourth, or about 22 miles, is within the boundary of Cuyahoga Valley National Recreation Area. The surrounding 32,000 acres of CVNRA are a microcosm of northeast Ohio, both in human and natural history. The national recreation area, the latest chapter in the valley's history, was created in 1974 through the combined energies of citizens and legislators, all with a strong desire to preserve and protect the green, open space, along with the recreation opportunities and the rich history of the valley. It was created at a time when the National Park Service was seeking to bring parks closer to people and is one of several such urban national recreation areas. CVNRA is now all of northeast Ohio's "back forty" for everyone to enjoy.

CVNRA is a unique park: within its bounds are federally-owned land, privately-owned land, and reservations owned and operated by Cleveland Metroparks and Metro Parks, Serving Summit County, all partners in managing the public areas. In this guide, we describe all the trails within the boundary of the national recreation area, including those managed by the metropolitan park districts. In doing so, we have put in one place information on over 125 miles of trails in the Cuyahoga Valley, hoping to clarify the many choices available to you for hiking, skiing, bicycling, and horseback riding. With guidebook in hand, you can plan your outings, from a short lunch-time walk to an all day trek.

The trail system in CVNRA is actually a "work in progress." In the early 1980s, the founders of the Cuyahoga Valley Trails Council (CVTC) assisted the National Park Service (NPS) at CVNRA in exploring the valley's existing and potential trails. The result of this joint effort was the National Park Service's *Trail Plan and Environmental Assessment* (1985) for Cuyahoga Valley. Every month CVTC volunteers do a work project to help maintain and improve the existing trails and construct new trails in accordance with the Trail Plan. Of the 115 miles of proposed trails about 24 miles have been completed, some by NPS staff and some by volunteers, and additional miles are under construction. We will revise this guide periodically as new trails are added to the system, and we encourage you to be a part of this progress by volunteering your time and talents to the volunteer work crews.

In this guide, we have grouped the trails geographically, north to south. For each trail, you will find a map and description and directions for reaching the trailheads shown on the trailhead map at the back of this book. The maps are oriented with north up, unless otherwise indicated with a north directional arrow. The first few lines of the trail description offer an overview of the trail's general character and special attributes. The difficulty rating is, of course, subjective, however we have taken into account the distance covered and the steepness and frequency of climbs—the shorter and flatter the trail, the easier. In the case of skiing and horseback riding, our ratings assume some beginning competence in controlling your skis or horse. We also note facilities located at the trailheads, using universal park symbols. Where there are a number of trails in one area, we suggest you read the general information on the area first, then refer to the particular trail you are interested in. Our guide will be most helpful when used along with CVNRA's free "Official Map and Guide," available at CVNRA visitor centers.

Our route descriptions are meant to keep you from getting lost by highlighting the general route of the trail and making note of intersections or confusing spots. If the trail is circular, we note in which direction it is described. Once you are familiar enough with the trail, try it in the opposite direction. You'll be surprised how different it looks! This is not advised on one-way ski trails, however. In those cases, the trails are laid out in one direction to make the best use of the terrain and ensure safety and a sense of solitude on the trail.

Keep in mind that the soils in this valley, some of which are loose deposits of glacial material, are unstable and "flow" when saturated. Flooded streams can erode banks and deposit trees where they weren't a day ago. The valley is always changing, and this means the trails can be changing too. What we describe today may be a little different when you go out to hike.

We hope that in presenting all these trail options to you, it will help in dispersing use throughout the valley. Some familiar areas can become crowded on beautiful summer weekends, stressing the natural resource and visitors alike. This can be avoided by a little advance planning and seeking the lesser-known areas on busy days. The effects of heavy use in an area are obvious and detract from your experience. You can help minimize your effect on an area by a few simple considerations: please carry out all trash (food refuse left in receptacles at the trailheads tends to get redistributed by scavenging animals), leave the radio at home, control your pets on a leash, and stay on the trail.

In our trail descriptions, we also point out historic features, plants, and animals which you might find along the trail, especially those unique to or well-represented in that area. We cannot be all-inclusive, but instead we try to bring your attention to a portion of the the rich natural life and cultural history in the valley and hope to whet your appetite for learning more. You will find in your ventures that your pleasure increases as you become more and more aware of the other lives that share this piece of the planet.

THE FOOTSTEPS BEFORE YOU

Before you begin exploring the trails, we would like to tell you some things about this river valley. As you follow the trails of the Cuyahoga Valley, you will be following paths that have seen many other feet before yours. Evidence of human habitation here goes back to about 10,000 B.C., following the last glacial retreat. The glaciers, which had covered the area with ice off and on, 2 to 3 million years ago, ground down and rearranged the hills and drainage patterns. The last glacial retreat exposed a drainage divide, separating the waters that flow to the Gulf of St. Lawrence from those that flow to the Gulf of Mexico. This is the same divide that causes the Cuyahoga River to make a U-turn half-way along its circuitous course from Geauga County to Lake Erie.

Following that last glacial retreat, prehistoric Native Americans hunted mastodons and mammoths. After these early peoples, other native populations emerged, surviving off the rich resources of the river and Lake Erie, and eventually farming and coming together in small villages. Throughout these many years, plant life evolved to the point that the area was covered by a dense, unbroken forest of massive trees. Some of the sycamores along the river were so huge that their hollowed trunks were used for shelter.

The first white explorers, followed by settlers, arrived in this valley in the late 1700s. Following the Revolutionary War, surveying parties made their way to the mouth of the Cuyahoga to begin to measure and map an area known as the Western Reserve. The Western Reserve, stretching 120 miles west of the Pennsylvania border and between the 41st parallel and Lake Erie, was land retained by the state of Connecticut when it surrendered the rest of its land claims to the young federal government. Connecticut then sold the wilderness reserve to the Connecticut Land Company to divide up and sell to eager easterners, both settlers and speculators.

The Cuyahoga River valley was truly "the West," and witnessed a typical phase of pioneering. In 1800, there were 24 million acres of seemingly unlimited forest in Ohio. Seeing these forests as an impediment to raising crops and livestock, the early settlers embarked on an intense cut and burn campaign, not unlike what is happening in South America today. By 1883, the forest cover was reduced to 4 million acres. If you look at canal-era pictures of the valley, you see mostly bare hillsides.

The early settlers could subsist, but could not progress economically without a means of transporting agricultural products to eastern and southern markets. The canals were a short-lived but successful solution: the first section of the Ohio and Erie Canal was opened in July of 1827, connecting Akron to Cleveland, and by 1840, Ohio led the nation in agricultural production.

The white settlers had other effects upon this land besides transforming forests to farm fields. They quarried stone, then later made use of sand and gravel for concrete building materials. They eradicated predators (at one time there were bears and mountain lions in the valley) and hunted fur-bearing animals, extirpating the beaver. Industries developed and grew, and the towns of Akron and Cleveland began to spread out towards each other.

Beginning around the 1920s, some Ohioans began to value the Cuyahoga Valley in a different way. Seeing an oasis of green between the two industrial cities, they began a conservation movement centered mostly on creating metropolitan park districts. A number of these early conservationists were private citizens who owned large retreats in the valley and wished to see them preserved for public use and enjoyment. Their pioneering preservation efforts led to the establishment of our exemplary metropolitan parks, and eventually to the creation of Cuyahoga Valley National Recreation Area.

THE NATURAL VALLEY TODAY

The deforestation trend that occurred in the Cuyahoga Valley during pioneering times has been reversed, and the valley now supports a diverse wildlife population owing to the variety of habitat types and the many "edges" between forest, field, stream, and wetland. The forests today are second and third-growth, different from the virgin oak, beech-maple, and pine woods. Today we have over 100 species of trees, including red maple, tulip tree, ash, wild black cherry, mixed oaks, and hickories, amongst the beeches. Dry uplands are dominated by oaks, while along the river bottoms you find sycamores, willows, cottonwoods, and Ohio buckeyes. The ravines hold relics of the cooler post-glacial period, such as eastern hemlock.

Birds and Beasts

The diversity of habitats in CVNRA makes the area one of the best in the state for birdwatching. Of the 230 or so bird species that have been found in the valley, several especially prefer this area of the state. One is the elusive veery. You may not see it, but are fortunate if you hear its ethereal, flutelike song. The woodcock is another—famous for its spiralling mating display performed in early spring. Turkeys were gone from the valley, but have been reintroduced in the area, and now are seen occasionally, though they too are quite secretive.

Your chances of observing other wildlife are quite good, especially if you take some care in your efforts. The best times are early morning or evening. For the best advantage, be quiet, go slowly, and even better, sit still. You won't see wolf or elk, but you could see a beaver working on its dam, or a fox or coyote stalking prey. White-tailed deer are plentiful. Raccoons, opossums, skunks, and bats are most active at night.

Along with the forests and meadows, your treks will take you through or past wetlands, including streams, floodplains, beaver marshes, and many man-made ponds. These wet habitats are where you can find one of our largest birds, the great blue heron, plus kingfishers, Canada geese, and wood ducks. Several species of native frogs, salamanders, reptiles, and amphibians moving and mating amongst the cattails and willows are just part of the highly productive wetland world.

Any time of the year, something is happening in the valley, but spring sets the fastest pace. In an astoundingly brief time period, from late March to early June, the valley is transformed from its open, sparse, grey, winter look to a dense, lush, emerald garden. In the midst of this transformation is a window of time in which dainty spring wildflowers bloom. It is also about this time that migrating birds pass through the valley, resting and feeding for a while once insects begin to hatch. The co-occurrence of warblers and wildflowers in early May strains the best of naturalists, worn out by gazing up, then down, up, then down.

In summer, animal activity appears to slow down, especially midday. Early morning, before the mist has burned off, and late evening when the insects and tree frogs begin their serenades, are good times for experiencing summer in the valley. Autumn brings the bittersweet excitement of change and cooler weather, along with the animals' preparations for winter. The height of fall color occurs about mid-October, a popular time for taking to the woods again for the sheer beauty of the scenery. Again, you may sight unusual birds in the valley as they migrate south to wintering grounds.

More and more visitors are discovering that winter offers its own special rewards to those who venture out. The starkness and silence are a welcome contrast to the fullness of the leafed-out seasons. You can observe animals by following their signs left in the snow, and given enough snow, you can enjoy the exhilaration of gliding over familiar terrain on skis. There are even special field guides to help you identify plants, trees, fungi, birds, and animal tracks during the winter months.

Rock-hard Facts

For those of you who love rocks, the geology in this area tells the valley's history in deep layers of time. Some of that history is buried far beneath the surface in shales formed from muds deposited in shallow seas 375 million years ago. These Devonian Period deposits are exposed in places where the Cuyahoga River has cut through the layers. Above these are Mississippian shales and sandstones, 330 million years old. The sandstones resist erosion, and when softer rock underneath is eroded, the sandstones sheer off to form cliffs such as those along Tinkers Creek. On top of these layers are the shale, sandstone, and conglomerate laid down in the streams and swamps of the Pennsylvanian Period. These form the surface bedrock wherever they are not overlaid by the younger glacial till. Sharon Sandstone and Conglomerate compose the familiar rock ledges of the valley.

After these Pennsylvanian Period deposits there is a long gap in the geologic record in Ohio—a gap of about 225 million years! In the Rocky Mountains, there are layers of rocks created during that time period, but not in Ohio. It is believed that during this time Ohio was undergoing extensive erosion, up until about 2 million years ago when climate changes spawned enormous polar ice caps which spread southward as glaciers.

These frozen masses, 1,000 to 8,000 feet thick, moved across northern Ohio like giant bulldozers, advancing and retreating in several different ice ages, with the most recent entering Ohio about 25,000 years ago. By the end of their final retreat, they had altered the landscape tremendously, in a scale difficult to imagine. Glaciers changed the course of streams and created new hills, called kames, by depositing tons of till (soils and ground rock). The Cuyahoga River today follows a course that is partly ancient, and partly altered by the glaciers. Underneath part of the Cuyahoga Valley, buried by 500 feet of till, sand, and silt, is a much older valley.

Bedrock in Canada is often exposed over large areas, but here it is only seen in knobs or ledges, and is usually buried by glacial deposits brought down from Canada in the ice sheets. Every time you find a boulder in the valley, you are finding a piece of Canada, usually composed of granite or granite gneiss, brought here during the ice age. In fact, the larger the boulder, the farther away it is from its source.

Animals were plentiful along the edge of retreating glaciers, but these animals were quite different from what we see today. Known as megafauna, these included giant mammoths, beavers, mastodons, and saber-toothed tigers. They are now all extinct. The vegetation changed within a few centuries from predominantly needle-bearing trees to the present day broad-leaved trees. A few of the cooler climate plants still remain, usually found in the cooler ravines.

Time to Get Going

We have mentioned only a few of the many species of plants and animals you may find here and simply highlighted the natural and cultural history. This is meant to get you started on a long and enjoyable period of exploration. To learn more, stop at the visitor centers in CVNRA. There you will find rangers leading guided walks, exhibits on the natural and cultural history of the park, an introductory slide show, a schedule of programs, general information, and book stores with field guides and local history. Canal Visitor Center is located on Canal Road at Hillside Road. Happy Days Visitor Center is located on State Route 303 less than a mile west of State Route 8. In addition to these, Cleveland Metroparks operates the Brecksville Nature Center, and Metro Parks, Serving Summit County has the Seiberling Naturealm just outside the southern park boundary. (See appendix for addresses and phone numbers).

The Cuyahoga River valley holds many surprises. There are those who have repeatedly tramped these "fuzzy green hills", to borrow a phrase from Edward Abbey, and on each return find something new and exciting. We invite you to discover your own special places in the Cuyahoga Valley.

BEFORE YOU HEAD OUT

What to Wear, What to Take

Before you go hiking in Cuyahoga Valley National Recreation Area, guidebook in hand, remember "if you don't like Ohio weather, wait a few hours, it will change!" All kidding aside, we forget that weather changes by the hour, not the day, so prepare for these changes before you set out. John Muir was known to set off into the Sierra Mountains with just some tea and bread, but most of us are far less tolerant of discomforts than he. A few select items in a daypack or fannypack can help ensure a pleasurable day.

First determine the time you will be out—all day or a few hours. The longer you are out the more protection from changing weather you will require, but even short hikes require a few basics to keep you comfortable and safe.

There are 14 basic items that provide you with comfort and protection from almost anything on hikes from five to fifty miles. These essentials include: lightweight shell top and bottoms (or a poncho in a pinch), gloves, balaclava or hat, spare socks, down vest (or midweight wool shirt), sunglasses, sunscreen, bug repellent, flashlight, lighter, map and compass, one quart water bottle, snacks, and a small personal first-aid kit.

A lightweight shell top and bottom of a waterproof-breathable fabric (such as Gore-Tex) provides the ideal protection for you, doubling for wind and rain protection in one garment. Though the temperature may seem warm, a quick rain shower and no protection leaves you wet and chilled. At this point you are a prime candidate for hypothermia. Remember that the majority of cases of hypothermia occur in temperatures of 30 to 50°F.

If additional warmth is required, slip a down vest or wool shirt under your shell jacket. A little wind goes a long way to chilling you. With a temperature of 40° F. and a wind of 15 MPH, the wind chill factor is 25° F. Gloves and a hat will help keep your extremities warm. A balaclava (a stocking type cap that can be worn as a hat or pulled down over the face and neck for added protection and warmth) will do the duty of a hat and scarf in cold weather and offers more versatility.

Abundant precipitation in this temperate climate creates a phenomenon which you will come to know, and perhaps even tolerate—mud. Mud is prevalent almost any time of the year, especially where the soils do not drain well—in the stream valleys and even on some of the high ground. Take care to wear adequate footwear, and carry spare socks. A change of socks half-way through a long hike will help prevent blisters on tender feet, and is a good excuse for a rest stop! If your feet do get wet, the change of socks will feel especially welcome. Also, some people find that wearing a thin pair of liner socks under heavier socks helps prevent blisters.

Sunglasses lessen eye strain and help reduce the cutting effect of winds on your face. Eye strain can drain your energy reserves quickly. Protection for your skin is also important: sunscreen and insect repellent should be included in your bag.

One quart of water and some high energy snacks (dried fruits, nuts, sandwich) will help keep you going. Choose foods that give quick energy boosts such as items high in carbohydrates and sugars. Many of the trailheads in the Cuyahoga Valley <u>do not</u> have drinking water, and even where there is water, the supplies are shut down in winter, so carrying water is especially important. When hiking, remember that even if you don't feel thirsty, it's a good idea to take frequent drinks to prevent dehydration.

Unless you are familiar with the trail, take along a map and compass. A small flashlight may come in handy if lost, for map reading in the dark, or locating trail markers. Your first-aid kit should include items for blister care, for minor cuts and scrapes, and some aspirin. These items take little space but can make a big difference if needed.

There is not a lot of space in a daypack, so choose clothing with minimal bulk. When hiking in warm weather, make sure there is room for clothing you may remove after you start. As long as you are moving you generate more heat, but when you stop to rest or enjoy the view, you may need an extra layer for chill protection. Remember it is better to be prepared than to get caught short.

Trail Etiquette and Safety

Proper trail etiquette promotes good trail safety; the two go hand in hand. Due respect between all trail users is a wise investment and the returns include a pleasant, enjoyable, and safe trail outing.

The most common type of trail where different types of users will meet is on an multi-use trail, although most trails do have more than one use. Therefore a review of some of the common-sense points of etiquette is essential.

Multi-use Trails

- Travel in a normal traffic pattern as on a regular roadway.
- Bicyclists should always voice their presence and what they are going to do when approaching a slower moving user, especially when passing from behind (for instance, "passing on your left").
- In winter, cross-country skiers should do the same.
- If possible, get off the trail or as far to the right of the trail as possible when stopping.

Bridle Trails

- Horses are like people. They all react differently in any given situation. Always bear this in mind when using a bridle trail for any purpose other than horseback riding.
- When encountering a horseback rider, stop, step off the trail, and let him pass. Ceasing activity will prevent any sudden noise or movements that may cause the horse to shy. Stay away from the horse unless the rider invites you to approach him. When the horse has passed, continue on your way.
- Horseback riders should voice their presence if not seen when approaching another trail user.

Cross-country Ski Trails

- When hiking, the main point of courtesy that should be practiced on trails designated for cross-country skiing is to avoid walking in the ski tracks. Footprints in the tracks make a more difficult time for the skier. Walk to the side of the trail, out of the tracks.
- Skiers should voice their presence if not seen when approaching another user.

In General

- Be aware of others who will be encountered on the type of trail you are using.
- Be aware that you, your equipment, and animals with you should be under control. Keep dogs on a leash, horses under control, and any equipment in top condition. Avoid excessive or uncontrollable speed on bicycles, horses, and skis.
- Stay only on trails which permit your use.
- When trails approach private property, please respect the landowner's privacy.
- Pack out trash: garbage placed in trailside containers tends to get strewn through the woods by scavenging animals.

With trail use on the rise, recreational enthusiasts will experience increased interaction between all trail users. Good attitudes and actions on the trail are indeed an investment—in safety—in camaraderie—in future enjoyment of the trails.

Longer Hikes

Several opportunities exist to combine sections of various trails in order to make longer loop hikes. The following are a few suggestions:

Combine a part of the Buckeye Trail with a part of the Towpath Trail. Two loops can be made this way, both starting at Red Lock Trailhead. Hike north on the Towpath

Trail from Red Lock until it meets the Buckeye Trail at Station Road. At this point, follow the Buckeye Trail west, then south, through Brecksville Metropark. When you reach Snowville Road, follow the connector trail back to the Red Lock Trailhead. Round trip distance is about 10 miles.

The second option, leaving from Red Lock, is to walk south on the Towpath Trail until you reach Boston Mills Road. Here you intersect with the Buckeye Trail which follows Boston Mills Road at this point. Follow the Buckeye Trail west, across Riverview Road, and into the woods. Continue on the Buckeye Trail to Snowville Road. At Snowville, follow the connector trail back to Red Lock Trailhead for a total distance of about 8 miles.

A third loop can be made by also starting at Red Lock Trailhead. Follow the Towpath Trail north until you reach Old Carriage Trail. Turn right (east) onto Old Carriage Trail and follow it until you reach the connector trail to the Bike & Hike Trail. Follow the connector to Holzhauer Road, then Holzhauer Road to the Bike & Hike Trail. Turn right (southeast) onto the Bike & Hike, and follow it to and along Brandywine Road. When you reach Stanford Road, turn right (you will pass Brandywine Falls Trailhead), and go about one-half mile until you reach Stanford Trail, intersecting to the left. Follow the Stanford Trail, eventually passing the Stanford AYH Hostel, and cross Stanford Road. The trail ends at the Towpath Trail. Turn right (north) and follow the Towpath Trail back to Red Lock Trailhead. Round trip is about 8 miles.

Several trails may be combined in the Kendall Lake Area to make longer loops. Studying this guide may give you some ideas, but here are a few suggestions: combine Salt Run Trail and the Cross-country Trail for about a 7-mile hike. Combine Ledges Trail with Pine Grove or Forest Point trail. You can add Haskell Run Trail or even Boston Run Trail to this combination for an even longer hike.

Other combinations may also be possible; these are just a few to whet your appetite. Study this guide to see if you can find any more combinations.

Off-trail Hiking

In the valley you'll find old road and animal trails that cross or come near the official trails. There are also picturesque ravines that offer their own little rewards, some even with delightful waterfalls. The temptation to go off-trail sometimes gets overwhelming—that enticing animal trail that follows down the ridge, that old roadway that goes up the edge of the gully. But, if you decide to follow this whim, there are several things to think about.

Metro Parks, Serving Summit County, has a strict policy of staying on official trails. Their annual ranger-led Stream Stomp is an exception to this policy. Elsewhere, be aware that you may be straying onto private property, and must take care to not trespass. If in doubt, ask permission to pass through a particular area. At all times, please remember that you are sharing this wonderful valley with many other creatures who call it home. Move carefully to minimize disturbance to vegetation or to nesting or resting animals. In stressful weather, disturbing an animal could jeopardize its survival.

Also, be careful! There are obstacles in the woods—fallen trees, multi-flora rose briars, poison ivy, stinging nettles, stumps, and holes, to name just a few. Waterfall and stream bed exploring has its own set of hazards including slippery footing. Go prepared: dress to protect yourself against insects and unfriendly plants.

And please, don't get lost. If you leave the trail, go prepared with a map and compass, and know how to use them. There are excellent books on learning the use of map and compass, and the North Eastern Ohio Orienteering Club specializes in cross-country map and compass exploring. You can purchase U.S. Geological Survey maps of the valley at the visitor centers. Most of the valley is shown on two maps, the Northfield and Peninsula Quadrangles. Be aware, however, that these do not show the public and private boundaries, so do some research before leaving the trails.

There are several areas in CVNRA that lend themselves well to cross-country exploring, and make good practice areas for learning to use a map and compass. In the northern part of CVNRA there is an area known as Terra Vista. It sits on a plateau above the corner of Tinkers Creek Road and Canal Road, and includes a couple of small fishing ponds and acres of shrubby, open area that was once a gravel pit operation. Further south, in central CVNRA, is the Kendall Hills area, acres of mowed hills, all interconnected, with splendid views across the valley. And in the southern part of the park, on Riverview Road just south of Bolanz Road, is the Indigo Lake area. Indigo is another good fishing pond surrounded by some open fields connecting to the Special Events Site.

Happy exploring!

THE TOWPATH TRAIL

The National Park Service (NPS) has undertaken the reconstruction of 19.5 miles of towpath within the boundary of CVNRA. When complete in 1994, the Towpath Trail will be the most important recreational trail in CVNRA. It will link Rockside Road in Valley View with Bath Road in Akron, following the historic route of the Ohio and Erie Canal. Some of the trail is complete now and much more is under construction. Let's travel into the future a few years to look into the past.

If you were to hike the entire length of the Towpath Trail in 1994, you would pass by, under, or over the remnants of a full range of canal related structures including: 16 locks, three aqueducts, two feeder canals, two arched stone culverts, and various weirs, sluices, overflows, gates, and other devices used to control water levels. Your trip would take you past much of the valley's human history such as Pilgerruh, site of the first known non-native settlement in the valley, some of the oldest homes in the region, a mill built on the canal to take advantage of the plentiful "free" supply of water power, the building that served as office for the Connecticut-based company selling shares in land in the Western Reserve, and villages that were once larger than Cleveland. Numerous other historic and prehistoric sites now invisible but historically important are located here as well. The Canal Visitor Center—with displays, exhibits, and programs—introduces 12,000 years of human history and development in the Cuyahoga Valley.

Signs of evolution of transportation would be found during your journey--the railroad line that helped put the canal out of business, an 1882 wrought iron bridge used for horse-drawn travel, the graceful form of a 1931 concrete arch bridge high above the valley floor, and signs (and sounds) of two major interstate highways whisking 20th century travelers from rim to rim with little clue of the history below.

In 1994, the Towpath Trail will connect a large number of trails, facilities, and other points of interest. In addition to Bedford and Brecksville Reservations, Deep Lock Quarry Metro Park, the Village of Peninsula, and the Stanford House AYH Hostel, you will be able to reach, via back roads or footpaths, Hale Farm and Village, Brandywine and Boston Mills Ski Resorts, Brandywine Falls, the Special Events Site (home of the Cuyahoga Valley Festival), Blossom Music Center, and Hampton Hills Metro Park. Along the way you might see deer, fox, skunk, and possibly even a beaver or turkey. Your travels would take you into some very diverse habitats of flora as well, so you would want to be on the lookout for beautiful wildflowers and unique and interesting plants. Actually, many of these things you are able to do right now! So let's get started.

Distances can be figured from mileposts, a convenient way to calculate mileages on linear structures such as canals and railroads. In this guide, distances will be given following the old canal system of measuring in miles from the beginning of the canal near the mouth of the Cuyahoga River in Cleveland's industrial "flats". Therefore, mile 12 is twelve miles from Cleveland's Flats.

The locks, on the other hand, were numbered beginning in Akron (Lock 1) and ending where the canal joined the river. Canal locks were always numbered starting from the high point, so Lock 1 is always at the highest point with lock numbers increasing as the canal travels downhill. The Ohio and Erie Canal, which ran 308 miles from Lake Erie at Cleveland to the Ohio River at Portsmouth had two high points, one of which was Akron. Hence, lock numbers in the Cleveland to Akron "flight" of locks increase as the canal heads north.

Please take note: much of the Towpath Trail is under construction. As a hiker, jogger, bicyclist, or skier you will notice that some sections of the trail will be marked **"Closed, 8 a.m. to 5 p.m."**or **"Caution—under construction—hazardous conditions may exist."** Please heed these signs. As time goes on, more and more of the Towpath Trail will be complete and available for all to enjoy.

Cuyahoga River South From Route 82 Bridge

1

6.25 miles

Hiking time:

3.5 to 4 hours

Bicycling time:

1.5 hours

Elevation change:

minimal

Easy to moderate

Towpath Trail
Rockside Road to Station Road

This section of the Towpath Trail follows the only watered section of the canal in the recreation area. Our description begins at Rockside Road, however, at present there is no convenient parking there. The closest parking lot is on Canal Road, just south of Stone Road at the site of the former Canal Visitor Center. Park here and walk about 100 yards north on Canal Road and cross the canal on the Stone Road bridge. Hike approximately .8 mile north to the starting point.

At the southern end of this section, parking will eventually be at the Station Road Bridge Trailhead. However, until this is constructed, we suggest you park in one of the small pull-offs near the east end of Chippewa Creek Drive at the Riverview Road entrance to Brecksville Reservation. Once completed, the Station Road Bridge Trailhead can be reached from Riverview Road, opposite the entrance to Brecksville Reservation.

Your journey begins at Rockside Road in Valley View (mile 11.2). Nearby, a tranquil Cuyahoga River makes its way north to Cleveland. Just beyond is the boarding site for the Cuyahoga Valley Line Railroad, an excursion train running on the historic Valley Railway. Soon the noise of traffic from Rockside Road recedes as you travel south back into a quieter, simpler time. In less than .3 mile is Lock 39, also known as 11- Mile Lock. Here you find the remains of a small metal bridge at the north end of the lock. This bridge was used by canalers to cross from one side of the lock to the other when the lower gates were open. Less than a mile further a road bridge crosses the canal on your left. Stone Road was so named as it was the road used to haul stone from the quarry nearby down to the canal for shipment. Across Canal Road is the majestic form of the Abraham Ulyatt House built in 1849 (private). This structure is one of the only remaining stone houses built in the Greek Revival style still extant in

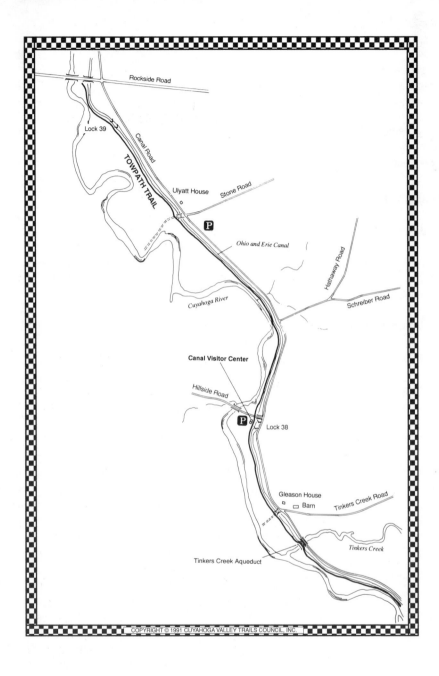

Towpath Trail — Rockside Road to Tinkers Creek

the Cuyahoga Valley. Do you suppose the stone came from one of the Independence quarries?

Just south of Stone Road and to the west (right) is a fence line marked by a line of trees. To the east, across Canal Road, is a small paved parking lot. Near here is thought to be the site of Pilgerruh, or Pilgrims Rest, where Moravian missionaries and their Christianized Indian followers built the first non-native settlement in the Cuyahoga valley in 1786. Although a historical marker erected further south places Pilgerruh near Tinkers Creek, the fields to your right are favored by most archaeologists.

Follow the trail south. Shortly after it swings slightly to the west (right) you see a bridge over the canal (Hillside Road). Soon the restored 1853 canal-era building located at Lock 38 comes into view. This is Canal Visitor Center, operated by the National Park Service. You may want to stop in and enjoy the canal exhibits on the first floor, including a working lock model, or learn more about human history of the valley from the excellent exhibits on the second floor. Picnic tables and restrooms are available here. (The hiking time from Rockside Road to the visitor center is about one hour.)

Take a moment to look over Lock 38 before resuming your journey. Although you have just passed mile 13, this lock was called 12-Mile Lock (do you suppose the canalers were superstitious?) In front of you is something that may seem quite simple, but was the evolution of many centuries of trial and error. Coming from Europe, this lock type, known as the two gate lock, is a remarkable piece of engineering. As you study the lock walls, you will notice two sets of indentations, one at either end. These held the wooden lock gates when open and allowed for passage of the canal boat without having the bulk of the gate restrict the lock chamber itself. On the downstream end (left, as you face the lock chamber) are iron straps anchored into the stone. These served as hinges for the massive timbers about which the gates pivoted. This lock is in good condition and perhaps soon will be fully restored to working condition. Maybe one day a restored canal boat will "lock through" on its way upstream or down. But for now, the trail beckons us on.

Just a few minutes south of the visitor center is Tinkers Creek Road. The bridge across the canal opposite Tinkers Creek Road once carried traffic from Riverview Road, but the bridge across the river was removed by the County Engineer. The canal bridge was closed to vehicular traffic but is still used today by hikers and fishermen. Just beyond, the canal and the Towpath Trail cross over Tinkers Creek (mile 13.7). This aqueduct, or bridge of water, is one of only 14 on the entire 308 mile stretch of Ohio and Erie Canal between Cleveland and Portsmouth, 3 of which were located on the 38-mile Cleveland to Akron portion. This one and the Mill Creek aqueduct (near 8-Mile Lock) are in use today.

To your left, on the hill above the intersection of Canal and Tinkers Creek Roads, stands the historic Edmund Gleason farm, marked by the huge red English style barn with its distinctive gambrel roof. The Greek Revival farmhouse was built in 1854 and features dressed sandstone. The barn was built in 1905 but no doubt replaced an earlier one, as most farmers built their barns first while living in simple cabins. Then, only after the farm began to prosper, would they improve their own dwellings.

After a gentle swing to the east (left) the Towpath again swings right and passes under Pleasant Valley/Alexander Road, bringing you to the only remaining mill structure along the watered portion of the canal. Alexander (now Wilson) Mill, at mile 14.6, was constructed in 1853 and used the excess or waste water which bypassed Lock 37 (or 14-Mile Lock) to power its grinding wheel. Used primarily for grinding grain, the mill used water power up until 1972 but switched to electricity as floating debris kept clogging the mechanism. Although they no longer grind at the mill, it remains a popular place to pick up feed and seed.

Immediately south of 14-mile Lock is a bridge on the towpath over a water control structure know as a waste weir gate. The matter of keeping just the right amount of water in the canal was a never-ending battle. Side creeks, leakage, animal holes, floods, and droughts all had to be accounted for, and a waste weir gate was one mechanism to drain excess water from the canal and drain the canal for repairs. This remains true today, as a steel mill in Cleveland's Flats still uses canal water and therefore must regulate its flow.

South of Lock 37, stop a moment to take in the view. The open pasture to your left, above Canal Road, represents what most of the area looked like 150 years ago. With a little imagination, you can erase the power lines in front of you and turn Canal Road into a narrow dirt path. Just down a piece and above this path sits the stately red brick Frazee house. This Federalist style house was finished in 1827. Along with the Jonathan Hale Homestead, it is one of the two oldest brick houses in the valley.

Cross two water control structures, and follow the Towpath along the canal in a gentle curve to the west (right). Here you enter a section of the Towpath Trail located far from any sound of humans. The Pinery Narrows, or simply the Narrows, is a secluded part of the recreation area protected by the close-in valley walls, through which only the canal, the river, and the Valley Railway can fit. Soon inside the Narrows the trail swings sharply to the east (left). This is Horseshoe Bend, or the Devil's Elbow (mile 15.5) so called for obvious reasons. This section is also open to horses; should you encounter someone on horseback, be courteous and step to the side to let them pass. The Narrows is a good place to spot wildlife. In mid-summer look for turtles sunning on a log; during a spring evening you might spot a blue heron silently tracing the river back to its roost at sunset. For the next few miles, travel quietly and see what you can find.

Soon the graceful arch of the Route 82 bridge, carrying traffic 145 feet above the Cuyahoga River, comes into view. It is one of the few remaining bridges which uses parabolic arches of reinforced concrete. Stop for a moment and look around. To

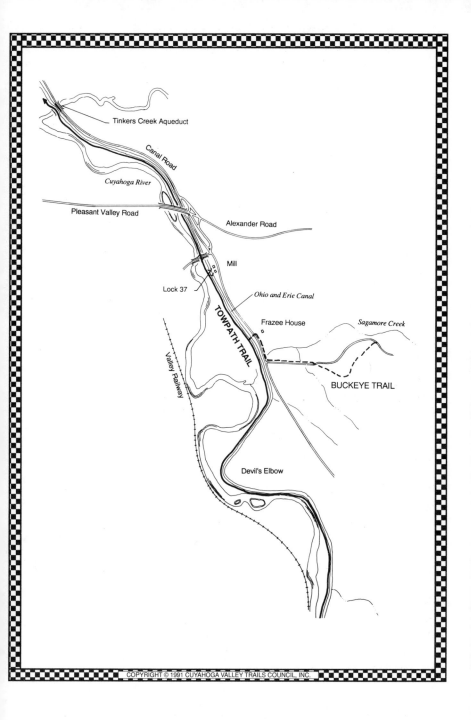

Towpath Trail — Tinkers Creek to Pinery Narrows

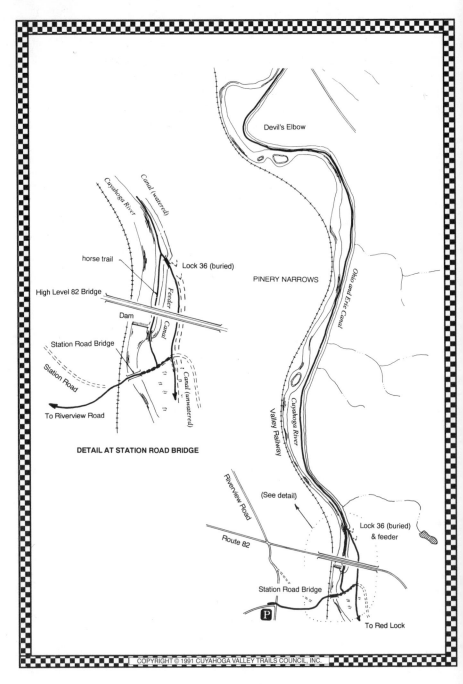

Devil's Elbow

PINERY NARROWS

Cuyahoga River

Canal (watered)

horse trail

Lock 36 (buried)

High Level 82 Bridge

Feeder Canal

Dam

Station Road Bridge

Station Road

To Riverview Road

Canal (unwatered)

DETAIL AT STATION ROAD BRIDGE

Ohio and Erie Canal

Cuyahoga River

Valley Railway

Riverview Road

(See detail)

Route 82

Lock 36 (buried) & feeder

Station Road Bridge

P

To Red Lock

Towpath Trail — Pinery Narrows to Station Road

your immediate right is the Cuyahoga River—300 years ago you may have seen the river used by a group of Delawares transporting furs. To your left is the canal—150 years ago, standing where you are, you may have had to move to let a team of mules pass. Far to your right are the rails of the Valley Railway—120 years back it would have been carrying goods and people up and down the valley faster than the canal. Ahead the Station Road Bridge crosses the Cuyahoga—80 years ago you would have seen it carry one of the first cars across the river. Today, you hear and see traffic on Route 82 above. Where else can you stand in one location and see over 300 years of the history of transportation?

Just north of the high-level bridge is Lock 36, or 17-Mile Lock (buried during the construction of the high-level bridge). Seventeen-mile lock is also the location of the Brecksville feeder canal and dam, one of three original feeder systems in the Akron to Cleveland stretch of canal. The main trunk canal is not watered from this point south. Follow the feeder canal to the river to see how the canal gets its water. If this is your roadhead, turn west (right) at the road and follow the blue blazes of the Buckeye Trail across Station Road Bridge, through the woods, to the entrance of Brecksville Reservation and your car. The distance along the Towpath Trail from Rockside Road to the parking area is 6.4 miles.

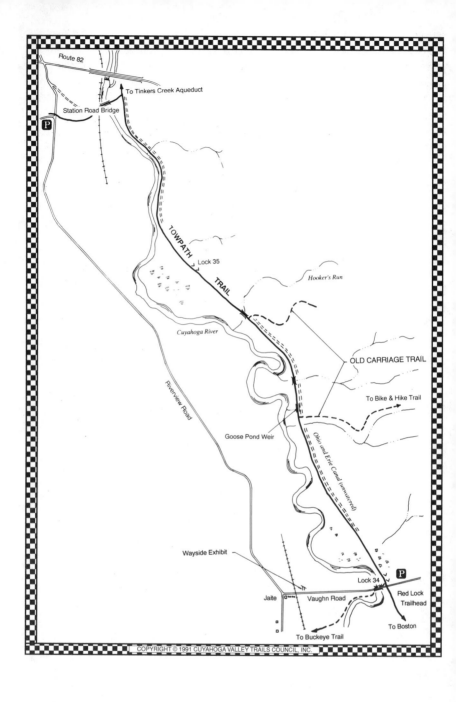

Towpath Trail — Station Road to Red Lock

2

Towpath Trail
Station Road Bridge to Red Lock Trailhead

2.7 miles

Hiking time:

1 hour-15 minutes

Bicycling time:

30 minutes

Elevation change:

minimal

Easy

Park for this section at Brecksville Reservation as outlined above for the Rockside Road to Station Road Bridge section. At the south end, park at Red Lock Trailhead on Highland Road.

South of Pinery Narrows, things change dramatically. Here the canal is no longer watered and the towpath, once a road in this section, is lined with trees on both sides. Hiking is easy and the trail allows good views of the river as it enters the slackwater behind the feeder dam just downstream of Station Road Bridge. Soon the river and canal part company as you head east (left) and approach Lock 35 (mile 18.4). Also called Kettlewell Lock, after the local canal resident, this lock was once near the site of a still. This gives Lock 35 its other nickname—Whiskey Lock.

After the Towpath Trail crosses Hooker's Run on a bridge, the northern connection of Old Carriage Trail (see page 88) takes off to the east (left). Ahead lies a section of Towpath Trail which is, in the estimation of some, one of the most beautiful stretches of the trail in the valley. Away from cars and commotion, this remote stretch of trail provides hikers, bicyclists, and skiers a chance to experience a piece of solitude and to watch natural habitats quietly reassert themselves after being displaced by the canal.

At mile 19.4, cross a wooden bridge built on the concrete remains of a water control structure sometimes called Goose Pond Weir, probably after the name given to a nearby pond. Immediately after is a small contemporary wooden bridge across the canal prism (the depression where the canal ran) marking the southern connection of Old Carriage Trail . Soon your trip on this section ends as traffic on Highland Road brings you back to the 20th

century. Just ahead are the remains of Lock 34, also known as Red Lock (mile 20.2).
The reason for this name is not entirely clear. Although the lock gates were one time
painted red, many gates were so painted, so why was this lock called "Red Lock"?
The condition of the remaining masonry is a testament to the early use of concrete as
a repair material. From 1905 to 1909, extensive repairs were made on the Cleveland
to Akron flight of locks as deteriorated stone was removed and concrete facing
applied. Eighty years of weathering have shown their effect. The parking lot is
reached by following the short trail to the left. Note the small concrete bridge that
carries you over the remains of the spillway around Lock 34.

Towpath Trail — Boston Lock

3

2.1 miles

Hiking time: 1 hour

Bicycling time:

30 minutes

Elevation change:

minimal

Easy

Towpath Trail
Red Lock Trailhead to Boston Trailhead

Two trailhead parking lots serve this section of the Towpath Trail. On the north is Red Lock Trailhead on Highland Road and on the south is Boston Trailhead on Boston Mills Road. The latter is just east of the trail and behind the foundation remains of an old barn. Both are well marked and easy to find.

The trail leaving the end of the parking lot takes you immediately past Lock 34 (Red Lock) to the Towpath Trail. A turn to the right leads to Old Carriage Trail (see page 88). Our journey begins by turning left, south, toward Highland Road. Immediately after crossing the road, look through the trees to your left. The small concrete structures just on the other side of the remains of the canal prism mark the beginning of the spillway for Lock 34. The spillway was a side channel used to carry excess water around the locks.

Just beyond, the Towpath Trail swings to the right slightly and joins the entrance road to the Jaite Mill. At this location (mile 20.4), Brandywine Creek slips almost unnoticed under the trail and road. Take a moment here to look at the graceful, arched stonework of the Brandywine culvert, to the east (left).

The Jaite Paper Mill was built in 1906 and used the plentiful supply of well water in the paper making process. The mill was one of the earliest industries in the valley, and the company town located about 1/4 mile west, built to house its workers and company officers, is used as CVNRA Headquarters today.

The next mile or so of trail carries you past beaver marshes and abandoned farm fields to Lock 33 (Wallace Lock). One-half mile later is the short connector to the Stanford Trail and Trailhead, and the Stanford Hostel, run

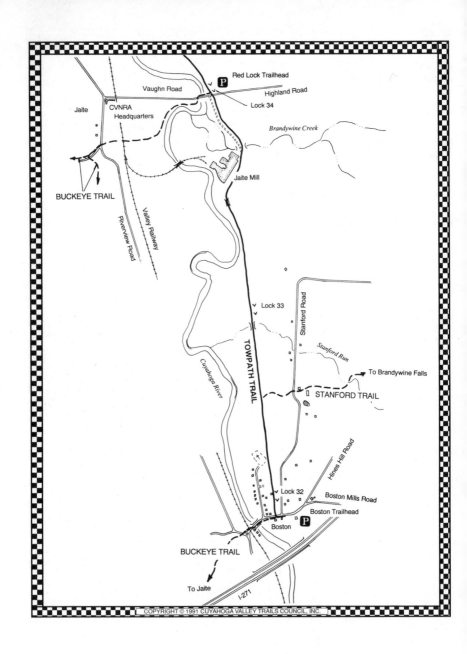

Towpath Trail — Red Lock to Boston

by the Northeast Ohio Council of American Youth Hostels. This is an excellent and attractive facility for groups, families, or individuals who wish to extend their stay in the valley overnight, at a moderate cost (see appendix). The 1.5 mile Stanford Trail (see page 93) has the 65-foot high Brandywine Falls as a scenic reward.

Continue south on the towpath and find another area flooded from beaver activity. Sharp eyes will be able to spot the beavers' home, or lodge. A small wooden bridge over Lock 32 (Boston Lock), mile 21.9, provides a good place to observe the lock and watch quietly for wildlife. On the east side of the prism you find the now familiar remnants of the concrete structure marking the spillway. On the main trail, you reach the canal town of Boston—the ending point of this stretch of 11 miles of canal Towpath Trail and the end, for now at least, of the section of Towpath Trail open to bicycling. The section of trail south, Boston to Peninsula, will be under construction soon and will be described in the next edition of this guide. The Boston Trailhead is about 75 yards to the east (left) down Boston Mills Road.

Towpath Trail — Boston

THE BUCKEYE TRAIL

When traveling from Cleveland to Cincinnati, most people follow I-71. Less well known routes comprise the Buckeye Trail, a 1200 mile path marked by blue blazes, which encircles the state of Ohio. Buckeye Trail Association, Inc., the group that supports the Buckeye Trail, is happy that the trail passes through the Cuyahoga Valley. These sections of Buckeye Trail are amongst the most scenic in the state.

Within the legal boundaries of Cuyahoga Valley National Recreation Area, the Buckeye Trail remains mostly off-road from its entry into Bedford Reservation near Egbert Road and Gorge Parkway to the intersection of Everett and Riverview Roads. The trail is along roads through the reconstructed covered bridge on Everett Road and past Hale Farm to permit those using the trail to enjoy these historic spots without straying far from the trail.

Whichever direction you follow the Buckeye Trail in the Cuyahoga Valley, north or south, Cincinnati is only 600 miles away. Along the way to Cincinnati, the trail traverses both glaciated and unglaciated terrain through Ohio's bluegrass country, its plains, and its hills. The trail passes over abandoned homesteads, strip mines, abandoned railways, towpaths of the historic state canal system, little-used country roads, levees, and even city streets. At present, about a third of the trail is off-road. The Buckeye Trail eventually will be part of a nationwide system of long distance trails, making it possible to walk by trail from the Cuyahoga Valley to the far corners of the United States.

Throughout the state, the Buckeye Trail is built and maintained entirely by volunteers. Except where the trail follows existing public trails or uses public land, no public assistance has been used to develop or promote the Buckeye Trail. Built primarily for hikers, the trail is open to all users without charge. However, users must determine and obey whatever rules are imposed by the landowner. Often the blue trail markers are regrettably faded almost beyond recognition. Sometimes in certain sections, the trail is overgrown or muddy. However, with some determination, adequate preparation, and trail guides, the hiker will experience great pleasures!

The 34 miles of Buckeye Trail within CVNRA are described in detail in the following pages. The route runs generally north and south, traversing the length of the Cuyahoga Valley from Bedford to Akron. In the heart of Brecksville Reservation is a major three-way intersection of the Buckeye Trail, where north, south, and west routes meet. It also marks the official site of the formal completion of the trail.

If you are out for a really long hike, or preparing for backpacking, the Buckeye Trail is ideal. In the Cuyahoga Valley you can link portions of the Buckeye Trail with other trails (such as the Towpath) or with sections of roads, to make long loop hikes. Suggestions of such loops are in the chapter "Longer Hikes."

Throughout its length, the Buckeye Trail is marked with blue blazes on trees and posts. At every trail junction, watch for the blue blazes to point the way. At any intersection where the trail changes direction, the blazes are positioned one above the other. The upper of the two is to the right or left of the lower, indicating which direction the trail turns. The only exception to this blazing is where the Buckeye Trail goes through land owned by Metro Parks, Serving Summit County. There the trail is marked by wood trail signs showing a blue BT in a directional arrow.

The Buckeye Trail Association, Inc., which maintains this trail, is a non-profit, tax exempt, all volunteer Ohio corporation organized and operated exclusively for charitable and educational purposes. The goal of the Association is to construct, maintain, and encourage use of the Buckeye Trail. For membership information and guides to the Buckeye Trail in other parts of Ohio, write: Buckeye Trail Association, Inc., P.O., Box 254, Worthington, OH, 43085.

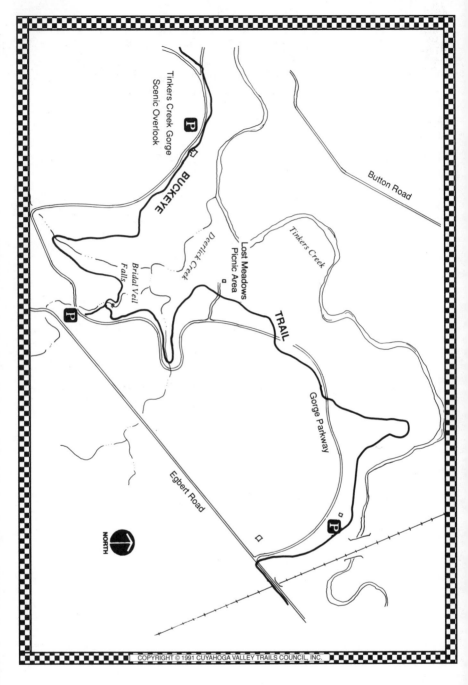

Buckeye Trail — Egbert Picnic Area to Tinkers Creek Overlook

4

**Buckeye Trail
Egbert Picnic Area (Bedford Reservation) to
Sagamore Grove Picnic Area**

6.1 miles

Hiking time:

3 to 3.5 hours

Moderate to difficult

Elevation change:

290 feet

The Buckeye Trail from Egbert Road to Alexander Road doubles as a bridle trail in some sections; in these sections it is wide, well-graded, with a gravel surface. From Alexander Road on, it is a narrow footpath. Hemlock ravines, waterfalls, rock ledges, and historic sites all combine to make this a favorite area for hiking or riding. The trail is linear, requiring you to double back or spot a car at the end.

The Buckeye Trail enters the northeast end of Cuyahoga Valley National Recreation Area near the intersection of Egbert Road and Gorge Parkway in Bedford Reservation. (See page 48 for more information on Bedford Reservation). The nearest parking to this east end of the reservation is at the Egbert Picnic Area on Gorge Parkway, just north of Egbert Road. There is additional parking at different points along the trail: Lost Meadows Picnic Area, Bridal Veil Falls, Tinkers Creek Gorge Scenic Overlook, a small lot at the corner of Overlook Lane and Egbert Road, the trailhead parking lot on Alexander Road, and at the Sagamore Grove Picnic Area. There are also restrooms and grills at the picnic areas. A ranger station and public restroom is located at the intersection of Egbert and Gorge Parkway.

The Buckeye Trail is described north to south. Begin this section of Buckeye Trail at the Egbert Picnic Area; the trail runs along the rim of Tinkers Creek Gorge, just behind the picnic shelter. Small access trails leave from the parking lot.

It is best to take the access trail to the right of the restrooms in order to not miss the spectacular views along the rim of the gorge. Turn left onto the Buckeye Trail, now following the blue blazes.

For a short way, a fence lines the edge of the trail between you and the steep-walled gorge. The trail then veers away from the fence and descends to meet up with a bridle trail. Bear to the left on the Buckeye Trail, joining the bridle trail. A short side trip in the other direction on the bridle trail takes you down to Tinkers Creek and the site of the old Powers Mill.

Back on the Buckeye Trail, a short uphill climb leads out to Gorge Parkway. Cross the all purpose trail and parkway to the south side of the road. Wind up and down along the golf course then again cross Gorge Parkway. About 500 feet beyond this crossing, a foot path leaves the Buckeye Trail, leading down to Lost Meadows Picnic Area. This is an interesting area to explore, with a pretty waterfall amongst the hemlocks.

Continue on the Buckeye Trail along with the bridle path, crossing the access road into Lost Meadows. At this point you enter a lovely area with beautiful hemlock ravines and views of Deerlick Creek and waterfalls to the right. The trail comes out to skirt the edge of Gorge Parkway, crosses over to the other side of the creek, and follows along the rim of the ravine.

Now about 2 miles from your start, you reach the steps coming down off Gorge Parkway leading to the Bridal Veil Falls Overlook. Cross Silver Creek on a pretty arched bridge. The overlook is to your right.

Follow the blue blazes on through a mature woods of oaks, hickories, and beeches, for about a mile. At this point you reach the Tinkers Creek Gorge Scenic Overlook into the 200 foot deep Tinkers Creek Gorge, a National Natural Landmark.

Past the overlook, the Buckeye Trail continues to just west of the intersection of Gorge Parkway and Overlook Lane. Cross the road to where the bridle trail again rejoins the Buckeye Trail. Here the trail bears away from the road to enter a deeply wooded area. Further along, follow the Buckeye Trail away from the bridle trail, turning sharply to the left, to visit an old quarry. Watch carefully for the blue blazes, following them around the quarry and back to the bridle trail. Shortly after this, now 4.2 miles from your start, you come to Egbert Road. There is a small parking lot off to the left just before you cross the road.

Across Egbert Road, continue to share the path with the bridle trail as both descend to the end of Egbert Road at Dunham Road. At Dunham Road, the Buckeye Trail uses the all purpose trail, turning to the left, parallel to Dunham Road. Very soon, however, the Buckeye Trail leaves the all purpose trail, crosses Dunham Road, then rejoins the all purpose trail at Alexander Road.

Cross Alexander Road, then continue south on the Buckeye Trail; here it uses the bike trail on an old railroad grade. In less than a third of a mile, watch for the point where the Buckeye Trail leaves the railroad grade to the west (right), dropping down onto a narrow footpath. This next mile of trail is especially scenic, following along the rim of Sagamore Creek. You can see two 25- foot waterfalls from the trail.

End this section where the Buckeye Trail comes out to Sagamore Road near the Sagamore Grove Picnic Area (there are restrooms and a shelter here).

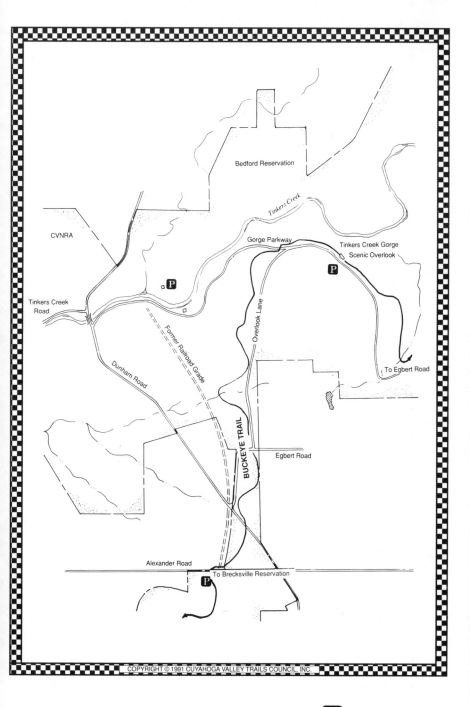

Buckeye Trail — Tinkers Creek Overlook to Alexander Road

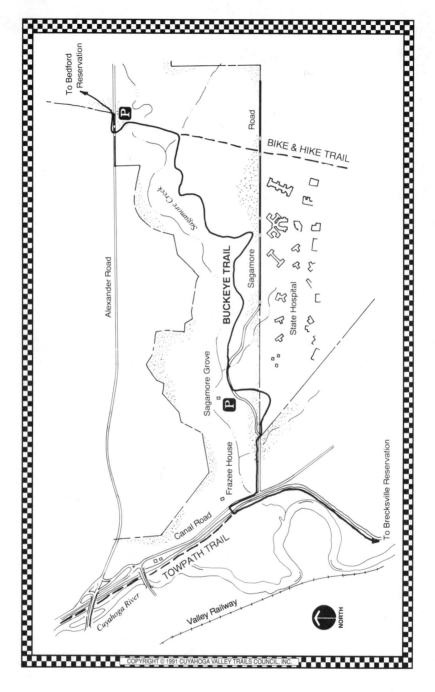

Buckeye Trail — Alexander Road to Sagamore Grove Picnic Area

5

Buckeye Trail
Sagamore Grove Picnic Area to
Brecksville Reservation

(See Towpath Trail map, pages 19-20.)

🚶

3.6 miles

Hiking time: 2 hours

Elevation change:

minimal

Easy

This section of the Buckeye Trail has two special attributes: it is almost entirely level, and goes through a unique roadless area of the valley known as Pinery Narrows, following the historic Ohio and Erie Canal towpath. Again, being a linear trail, the Buckeye Trail requires you to either drop a car at the opposite end or return on the same route. Double your allowance of hiking time for a round trip.

You can reach the north end of this section of Buckeye Trail by parking at the Sagamore Grove Picnic Area, on Sagamore Road, just north of Canal Road.

Leaving from the Sagamore Grove Picnic Area, cross Sagamore Road and follow the blue blazes into the woods (look carefully for the blazes), then in a short way come back out to follow Sagamore Road to the intersection with Canal Road. The Buckeye Trail turns north and follows Canal Road for a short distance. At the historic Frazee-Hynton House, built in the 1820s and predating the canal, turn left and cross the Ohio and Erie Canal, then left again to get onto the Towpath Trail which follows the old canal towpath.

The Buckeye Trail follows the Towpath Trail route to the south for the next 3 miles, some of the most favored miles along the canal. Hemmed by the Cuyahoga River on one side and the watered canal on the other, you can travel these miles undisturbed by road distractions. The hustle and bustle of canal days is far removed from today's quiet. Also missing are the majestic white pines that gave this area its name, Pinery Narrows. In the 1800s they were cut for masts and floated to Lake Erie for the Great Lakes' sailing ships.

At the southern end of this section, you reach the bottom of Pine Hill Road, which becomes Station Road on the other side of the river. Turn to the right (west) and cross the Station Road Bridge. At the time of this publication, there are plans to construct a trailhead at Station Road. For now we suggest that to complete this section of Buckeye Trail, you continue following the blazes a short distance out to Riverview Road. Just across the road is the entrance to Brecksville Reservation—several small parking areas are located here near the intersection of Riverview Road and Chippewa Creek Drive. If you are continuing on the Buckeye Trail, stay on Riverview Road and turn left (south) to follow the blazes up Riverview Road. The trail reenters the woods just up the road and begins a beautiful, meandering tour through the lesser traveled areas of Brecksville Reservation.

Buckeye Trail Crossroads — Brecksville Reservation

6

Buckeye Trail
Brecksville Reservation
to Red Lock Trailhead

7 miles

Hiking time: 3-4 hours

Elevation change:

200 feet

Difficult

In this section, the Buckeye Trail continues as a narrow footpath. It leaves the river valley, climbs 200 feet towards the west rim of the valley, wanders through much of Cleveland Metroparks Brecksville Reservation, then traverses several stream ravines before descending again to the valley floor. It is marked throughout the length by blue blazes painted on the trees.

To reach this section from the north, park in Brecksville Reservation near the eastern entrance at Riverview Road and Chippewa Creek Drive. This being a linear trail, you need to arrange to leave a car at the other end, or return on the same route. Or, if you are in the mood for a long loop hike, you can return via the Towpath Trail. Parking at the south end of this section is at Red Lock Trailhead, on Highland Road, .5 mile from the National Park Service Headquarters at Vaughn and Riverview Roads. This section, like the other sections of Buckeye Trail in this guide, is described from north to south.

From the parking lot on Chippewa Creek Drive, walk out to Riverview Road and look for the blue blazes. The Buckeye Trail comes out of the woods that you see across the road and then follows the road. To go south on the Buckeye Trail, turn right onto Riverview Road, cross the creek, and go halfway up the hill until you find the blue blazes directing you into the woods. At this point the trail again becomes a narrow footpath and starts you on an interesting tour of the lesser traveled parts of Brecksville Reservation.

Begin the climb through mature woods; the first junction is My Mountain Trail, marked with orange markers. (For a side trip, you can follow My Mountain Trail .5 mile to a high knoll from which you can look back down on the valley.)

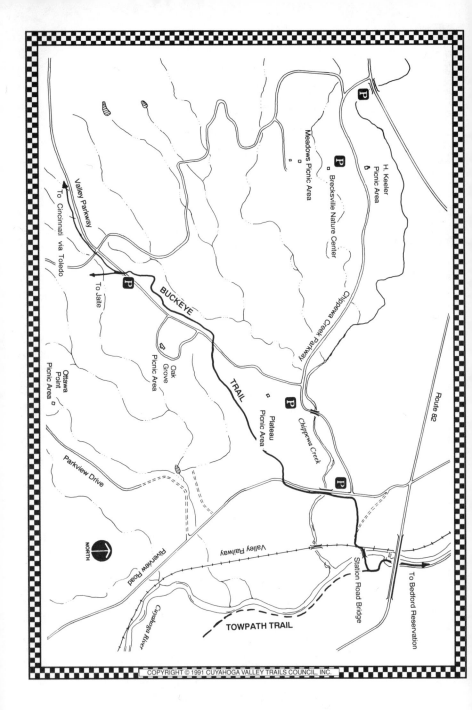

Buckeye Trail — Brecksville Reservation

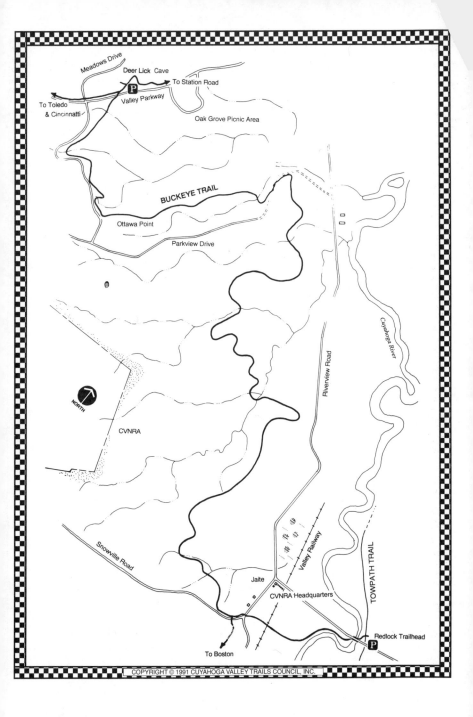

Buckeye Trail — Brecksville to Jaite

...inue southwesterly on the Buckeye Trail and cross Valley Parkway (Oak Grove Picnic Area is to your left). Here you are one mile from the start of your hike. Now on the north side of the road, follow the trail just below the level of the road, paralleling the road, until you come to the Buckeye Trail signpost. This 3-sided signpost shows you where you are in relation to the entire Buckeye Trail. It was donated by Cleveland Metroparks and also marks the spot where the Buckeye Trail was officially completed, linking all four corners of Ohio. If you continue west, you can reach Cincinnati in 441 miles; continuing south you can reach Cincinnati in 552 miles, and turning back and going north you can enter Mentor Headlands State Park after only 65 miles.

At this point, hopefully you can take some time to explore the Deer Lick Cave area. The Berea sandstone formation is just to the west of the signpost along the trail. Steps lead down into the cave area, rich with fern gardens and plush mosses.

To continue south on the Buckeye Trail, cross Valley Parkway, following the blue blazes. (The Buckeye Trail section heading west soon leaves the reservation.) The Buckeye Trail joins a bridle trail just across the road. Continue with this bridle trail for .7 mile. At the next major trail junction, the bridle trail crosses the road to go to the stables; stay on the Buckeye Trail on the east side of Meadows Drive. It narrows to a footpath again. You can see an abandoned quarry near the trail.

At the entrance to Ottawa Point Picnic Area, the Buckeye Trail joins the entrance road into the picnic area. This is a reservable area; if it is in use, please respect the privacy of the occupants. Follow the Buckeye Trail through the picnic area, then again pick up the footpath where the trail borders the edge of a field. Now you are traveling east before turning south again.

Beyond the picnic area, take the trail through a red pine plantation then descend to cross a creek. Follow the Buckeye Trail as it goes onto the alignment of old Parkview Road, then for about the next two miles you travel south again, climbing up and down several valleys. After two miles you reach a ridge near Riverview Road where you can enjoy superb views of the valley.

Beyond the ridgetop, follow the blazes into the fields, then in about .5 mile descend through the woods to a creek. Cross this creek several times, working your way towards Snowville Road. You come out into a meadow shortly before reaching the road. White-tailed deer frequent this area, and if lucky you might also catch a glimpse of a red fox or coyote.

At this point you have several options, depending on where you left a car and time constraints. To go further on the Buckeye Trail, cross Snowville Road. The next road crossing is at Columbia Road, 2.2 miles away. If you left a car at Red Lock Trailhead, or wish to return via the Towpath Trail, turn to the left on Snowville Road and then cross Riverview Road. Follow the blazes through the fields, out to Vaughn Road, then across the river to the trailhead. A round trip can be made by following the Towpath Trail back north (considerably flatter, faster, and shorter than your trip south). And of course your other option is to return on the same trail, which will look entirely different traveled in the other direction!

7

🚶

5.6 miles

Hiking time: 3 hours

Elevation change:

250 feet

Difficult

Buckeye Trail
Red Lock Trailhead to Boston Trailhead

The Buckeye Trail in this section continues as a narrow footpath. From the trailhead you climb to the west rim, then follow the trail as it continues to cross tributary creeks which flow into the Cuyahoga River. These side ravines and intervening woodlands are typical of the beautiful forested terrain of the Cuyahoga Valley. Blue Hen Falls, towards the southern end of this section, is a good destination for lunch, exploring, or photography. You can return along the same trail, retracing your steps, or use the Towpath Trail to make a long loop hike.

This small area is rich in local history. The northern trailhead, Red Lock, is named after Lock 34 on the Ohio and Erie Canal, located next to the parking area. Over 100 years ago the area would have been crowded and noisy as farmers brought their products to a loading basin near here to be transported to markets via the canal. After the turn of the century, paper maker Charles Jaite built a mill south of Highland Road along Brandywine Creek. In addition to the mill, he constructed a company town to house workers and the company store. Seven of the ten buildings remain and have been faithfully restored to their original appearances, including their banana yellow color. They now house the National Park Service headquarters for CVNRA. The Buckeye Trail also passes near the North District Ranger Station which is housed in a restored brick home built in the 1800s by Jonas Coonrad, one of the early prominent citizens of Brecksville. In addition to farming, he operated a cheese-making business here.

For access to this section of the Buckeye Trail, park at the Red Lock Trailhead on Highland Road, .5 mile from park headquarters which is at the intersection of Riverview and Vaughn Roads (Vaughn Road becomes Highland Road when it crosses the Cuyahoga River). Three-quarters of the way along this section there is a small parking area at Blue Hen Falls on Boston Mills Road, one mile west of Riverview Road. The southern trailhead for this section is the Boston Trailhead, located on the south side of Boston Mills Road just east of the village of Boston. There are portable toilets at these trailheads.

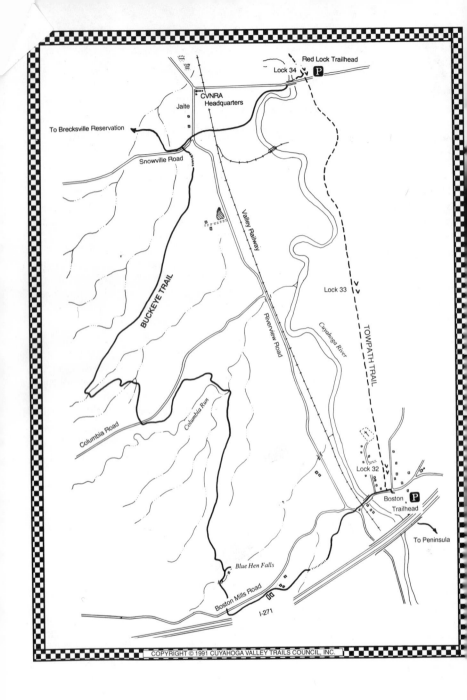

Buckeye Trail — Jaite to Boston

Beginning from Red Lock Trailhead, cross the river, then cross over to the south side of Vaughn Road and go south along the river and through the fields. This is a short access trail linking the trailhead with the continuation of the Buckeye Trail. Follow the blue blazes, which mark the Buckeye Trail throughout its length, under a powerline, across the railroad tracks, then across Riverview Road. Go about 200 yards up Snowville Road, then cross the road and enter the woods. Watch for the trail sign marking the turn.

Follow the blue blazes as the trail winds through the young woods, until you come to a set of steps built into the steep hillside. These steps were built in 1990 and 1991 by volunteers taking part in American Hiking Society Volunteer Vacations. Imagine what the climb was like before the steps! This climb takes you about 140 feet above the valley floor.

At the top of the hill, turn to the right and follow an old farm road along the ridge. Massive oak trees line the trail, with beech trees on the slope off to the right. When the leaves are off these trees there is a good view towards the south. There you can see the bright red barn and handsome brick Coonrad house, now the North District Ranger Station.

Just beyond a radio tower and block building, the trail comes out into the open, jogs left, then right. Watch for the blue blazes here when returning as it's easy to miss this jog.

This open area, created by utility corridors, is a couple hundred feet above the valley and is an especially good place for sighting hawks and turkey vultures soaring on thermals. Songbirds prefer the edge along the meadow and forest. It is worth it to have carried binoculars with you at this point. You can observe songbirds close by or enjoy the spectacular, long views.

After crossing the utility right-of-way, continue on an old one lane road through the oaks and maples. Watch for the cutoff to the left, following the blue blazes. Beech trees become more prominent as you cross a small ravine, then a larger, cool ravine, crossing the creek on stepping stones. Steps notched into the slope lead the way up the other side. The trail then widens again through fields and soon reaches Columbia Road.

Cross Columbia Road. The trail now parallels Columbia Road for a short distance, just below the level of the road. A hemlock ravine slopes off to the right. Further along, some foundation stones and large oak trees surrounding a clearing are all that remain of an old homestead. This area is owned and managed by Metro Parks, Serving Summit County.

Just after the clearing the trail begins to descend towards the ravine formed by Columbia Run. Thick green moss and graceful, evergreen hemlocks framing a small

...ng about 8 feet above Columbia Run make this an especially attractive spot. ...emlocks can be found in scattered locations throughout the state, but need a moist, cool environment such as these northern creek ravines.

Cross Columbia Run on stepping stones, then watch carefully for blue blazes pointing the way up out of the ravine. At the top, follow the ridge until you reach another utility right-of-way. Just after this right-of-way the trail drops down towards Spring Creek.

A side trail leads 100 yards to Blue Hen Falls. This falls, like others in the valley, drops over Berea Sandstone to the less resistant Bedford Shale below. Following the path along the stream downstream you can reach Buttermilk Falls, formed on Bedford Shale. By following streams this way, and observing the rock banks, you can see the layered rock of northern Ohio exposed like layers of a sliced cake.

Back on the Buckeye Trail, leaving Blue Hen Falls, cross Spring Creek on a wooden bridge, then follow the paved path to a small parking area and on across Boston Mills Road. Here the trail climbs the hill towards I-271. Follow the blue blazes through woods paralleling I-271, into an open field, then through National Guard property. Past the barracks and caretaker's house, follow the trail down a road and across a creek. After the creek, there is a set of 87 steps to take you back up to the ridge. Follow this ridge, then wind down a steep, and often slippery, hill ending at Riverview Road.

Cross Riverview Road and follow the blazes through Boston, crossing the Cuyahoga River and the Towpath Trail before reaching Boston Trailhead on the south side of the road. You can make a long loop hike by returning north on the Towpath Trail, which is all level.

8

🚶

4 miles

Hiking time: 2 hours

Elevation change:

240 feet

Moderate

Buckeye Trail
Boston Trailhead to Pine Lane Trailhead
(Peninsula)

This section of the Buckeye Trail is a narrow footpath on the east rim of the Cuyahoga Valley. It takes you through some terrain that has been altered by the construction of major highways, but also goes into undisturbed areas. Because of this, there is a wide variety of habitats along the trail, including old orchards, a borrow pit, mature oak woods, and the pristine Boston Run valley. Through these different areas, you can find an equally diverse collection of plants and animals.

Parking for the Buckeye Trail is at Boston Trailhead on Boston Mills Road, .1 mile east of Riverview Road. At the south end, is Pine Lane Trailhead: going east out of Peninsula on Route 303, watch for the trailhead sign indicating a left turn onto Pine Lane. The trailhead is down the road, on the right.

Starting from Boston Trailhead, find the trail by walking south (towards the 1-271 bridges) along a dirt service road. After going under the I-271 bridges, look for blue blazes directing you left and into the woods. Entering the woods, the trail climbs through an oak/hickory forest and an old apple orchard. Further along, you go through a beech/maple woods, then come out into a field along the Ohio Turnpike. Blue blazes on shrubs and trees lead the way away from the highway and back into the woods.

Follow the blazes in and out of grassy and forested areas until you reach Boston Mills Road. Turn right and follow Boston Mills Road for about 100 yards, then turn left into the woods, where the trail follows a beautiful ravine. Follow the blue blazes along the ravine, then back onto Boston Mills Road. Turn left to cross the bridge over the Ohio Turnpike. At the end of the bridge, turn right and climb the short hill into the woods along the highway.

Here you find a stand of white pines, a true sign of northern climes. They are easily identified by long, soft

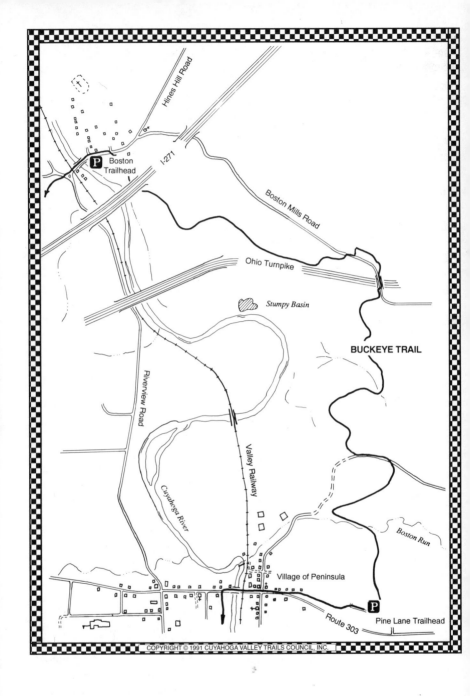

Buckeye Trail — Boston to Pine Lane

needles in bundles of five (five needles, five letters in w-h-i-t-e). Among the conifers, only white pines, eastern hemlocks, and tamaracks are native to this area. These pines were probably planted here, as they are in such straight rows.

A whole book could be written on these lovely trees; they, more than any other type of tree, starred in early white settlement of this continent, being used for everything from giant masts of sailing ships to homes, bobsleds, covered bridges, and roof shingles. When this country was first settled by Europeans, huge stands of white pines stretched for miles; an early pioneer saying declared that a squirrel could travel its lifetime without ever coming down from the pines. Our native stands in the valley are all gone. The widespread decimation of the native pines contributed to the start of the conservation movement. Now white and red pines, which are tolerant of low moisture and nutrient levels in soils, are planted in disturbed areas to hasten the restoration of forest cover.

Along the trail and to the right of these pines is a depression that was made when soil was dug for the Ohio Turnpike bridge embankments. This is an interesting area to explore for unusual plants such as the fringed gentian which blooms in the fall. Deer browse this area, and you can frequently hear field sparrows calling from the taller shrubs.

At the end of the pines, turn right (watch carefully for this turn—an old lane goes straight) and follow the trail through the oak woods along the south side of the depression, then bear left and cross two small drainages. An almost pure stand of young oaks is growing here. Continuing on, a small pond and former home site are to the right of the trail just before you reach Akron Peninsula Road.

Turn to the left, walking east along Akron Peninsula Road, and watch for the blaze and sign marking the point where the trail crosses the road and reenters the woods. This last mile of trail goes into and out of the Boston Run valley. This rich, moist valley is full of wildflowers in the spring: hepatica in delicate shades of pink or blue, trillium, toothwort, violets, and wild geranium are just a few of the flowers that can be discovered here. It is in woods such as these that you might also hear the flutelike song of the wood thrush or the clear, musical song of the hooded warbler, both elusive birds of northern woodlands.

A log has been placed across Boston Run for the crossing. You may prefer wading if the water level is low. After the steep climb out of the creek valley, follow the trail across a utility cut (the openings off the utility cut can be obscured in the dense growth of summer), then through a pine planting, and finally into the parking area at Pine Lane Trailhead. If you want to go into Peninsula, follow the blazes out of the parking lot and to the right down the lane and onto an old brick road. This was an earlier roadbed of Route 303; it joins the present Route 303 just east of Peninsula.

BEDFORD RESERVATION

Bedford Reservation is a unit of Cleveland Metroparks. The main natural feature of this park is beautiful Tinkers Creek Gorge, a National Natural Landmark. The reservation protects much of the dramatic gorge and in turn creates a delightful place to picnic, hike, ride horseback, or explore for waterfalls.

Tinkers Creek, the largest tributary of the Cuyahoga River, was named in memory of Joseph Tinker, a member of Moses Cleaveland's 1796 surveying party. Tinker was one of three men who died when their boat was capsized in a storm on Lake Erie. Tinkers Creek drops 90 feet in two miles, cutting a steep walled gorge from 140 to 190 feet deep. The inaccessibility of the gorge was a natural impediment to development in the 1800s, except for the more shallow upper gorge where numerous mills were built around the Great Falls of Tinkers Creek in Bedford. These mills ushered the industrial age into the area around 1820, while the rest of the gorge largely escaped timbering and development.

The upper Tinkers Creek Gorge used to be known as the Bedford Glens and was a destination for weekend outings as early as the turn of the century. A popular dance hall was part of Bedford Glens Park until 1944, when the hall burned to the ground ending that romantic era. The gorge first achieved official park protection when Cleveland Metroparks acquired 1300 acres in the 1920s, and later expanded it to 2154 acres.

This unique natural area has many tree and shrub species, an unmatched spring wildflower display, and carpets of ferns, mosses, lichens, and liverworts. Here geology is laid before you as the water-cut gorge exposes all the bedrock found in the valley. Delta-like deposits of red muds and offshore deposits of grey muds and silts constitute the Bedford Formation. Other formations that are exposed here are Chagrin, Cleveland, and Bedford Shales and Berea Sandstone. Winter transforms this gorge into an icy wonderland. The park's more than 70 cascades and waterfalls freeze into ice formations, some 30 to 50 feet high.

The scenic overlook on Gorge Parkway offers a vista (especially in the fall) that many claim is unrivaled anywhere north of the Smoky Mountains. Other attractions of this area include Bridal Veil Falls, Shawnee Hills and Astorhurst Golf Courses, several picnic areas and shelters, plus ballfields and playfields. The trails of Bedford Reservation are Bridal Veil Falls Trail, Hemlock Creek Loop Trail, bridle trails, the all purpose trail, and part of the Buckeye Trail (described in the Buckeye Trail chapter).

Numerous other informal trails have been used over the years as more adventurous visitors explored along Tinkers Creek and its tributaries discovering Bedford Reservation's hidden treasures. In some areas, trails that were constructed years ago are no longer formally used or kept in repair. One such trail runs along the north rim of Tinkers Creek and offers some beautiful views into the gorge, as well as access to hemlock-lined side creeks and small waterfalls. It is permissible to explore these informal trails, remember, however, they are not signed or maintained.

To reach Bedford Reservation from the west, get onto Dunham Road from Turney Road, Tinkers Creek Road, or Alexander Road. The entrance into the Hemlock Creek Picnic Area is at the intersection of Dunham and Tinkers Creek Roads, and Gorge Parkway is just across Tinkers Creek.

Gorge Parkway and Egbert Road provide access from the east. Egbert Road inter- sects with Broadway Avenue (Route 14) near the intersection of Routes 8 and 14 in Bedford. From Egbert Road, turn onto Gorge Parkway to enter the reservation. Parking is available at either end of the reservation; you can find additional areas along Gorge Parkway and at the Gorge Overlook and Bridal Veil Falls areas, and at Lost Meadows and Egbert Picnic Areas. Picnicking, grills, restrooms, water and shelter are available at the major picnic areas, and a Cleveland Metroparks Ranger Station is located at the east end of the reservation at the corner of Egbert Road and Gorge Parkway. Your options for hiking here are as varied as the many access points to them!

9

Bridal Veil Falls Trail

(See map, page 54.)

.25 mile

Hiking time:

15 minutes

Elevation change:

30 feet

Easy

This short trail is located off of Bridal Veil Falls parking area on Gorge Parkway, just east of Overlook Lane. A footpath and stairs leads you to several overlooks from which you can view the stream and Bridal Veil Falls.

To begin the trail, cross the road and descend the steps. Follow along the shale-bottomed stream, then cross the stream on a footbridge. Walk a short ways to the last observation platform, this one for viewing the falls itself. From here you can absorb the quiet beauty of the falls and surrounding hemlock ravines.

Part of the Buckeye Trail follows this trail on its way to the Tinkers Creek Gorge Scenic Overlook (about 1.5 miles further west). From Bridal Veil Falls, you can return to the parking lot via the same route, or continue onto the Buckeye Trail as your time and wanderlust permit. The hike to the Tinkers Creek Gorge Scenic Overlook passes through a mixed hardwood forest with a spectacular spring wildflower display. Round trip distance is about 3 miles.

10

.6 mile

Hiking time:

30 minutes

Elevation change:

minimal

Easy

Hemlock Creek Loop Trail

(See map, page 56.)

This short loop from Hemlock Creek Picnic Area offers you a taste of Tinkers Creek valley from the creek level. You can see the variety of vegetation created by the deep valley: hemlocks clinging to the north-facing slope of Tinkers Creek valley contrast with the oak forest on the drier south-facing side. In spring, you can find one of the lushest displays of eastern forest wildflowers in CVNRA. Large clumps of Virginia bluebells, wild geraniums, dog toothed violets (including an unusual white variety), phlox, trillium, bloodroot, and hepatica carpet the floodplain soils, a delight to amateur botanists. If your interest is geology, you can study the layered history of the valley exposed in the cliff walls. This is also an excellent spot for the birder. Bring binoculars and field guide!

Access to this trail is from the Hemlock Creek Picnic Area, located near the intersection of Tinkers Creek Road and Dunham Road, on the north side of Tinkers Creek. The trail begins beyond the ballfield.

To start the trail, walk away from the parking lots, close to the hillside on your left. Looking ahead and behind, you can see that this alignment used to be an old road. This was Button Road, which still exists at the top of the hill. It came steeply down into Tinkers Creek valley, and was used by farmers in the 1800s bringing goods to the valley and the Ohio and Erie Canal.

Follow this old road a short distance until the main trail bears to the right. The old road ahead is now just a narrow path. Bear to the right, approaching Tinkers Creek. The trail continues to circle to the right, paralleling the creek. An informal trail goes about 0.8 mile further upstream, but is no longer maintained. Nonetheless it allows you to explore a little further in this beautiful creek valley. If you take it, you will know when to turn around when you reach an impass-able place in the creek. At that point, return along the same trail to get back onto the loop trail.

Back on the main trail, you will find a couple of benches offering a chance to sit and observe. Continuing on the loop, you soon reach the shelter and parking lot where you began. Looking downstream from here you can see the remains of supports for the old Pittsburgh and Lake Erie Railroad (later New York Central, then Penn Central) trestle which crossed Tinkers Creek. High above, on the south side of the valley, you can see the promontory formed by the railroad embankments. The steel trestle was built in 1911, used until the 1960s, then dismantled in 1974. Imagine the scary thrill that many kids must have had, daring each other to cross The Trestle.

11

6 miles

Riding time: 2.5 hours

Elevation change:

270 feet

Moderate to difficult

Bridle Trails

Bridle trails cross the full length of Bedford Reservation, high on the south rim of the valley, and along the valley floor at the south end of the reservation. The trail is partially shared by the Buckeye Trail. Traveling these bridle trails, you can experience the best of what Bedford Reservation has to offer: deep woods, high ridges, hemlock ravines, Tinkers Creek valley, cascades, and waterfalls.

Trail riding has a long history in the reservation, dating back to the 1920s when the park established the first bridle paths and began using a mounted ranger patrol. You can still find some of the original rock work at culverts and retaining walls along the trails.

The trails are described from the lower (western) end of the gorge as this is where the best parking is located. One trail comes up from the creek to the rim, while the other stays at the higher elevation of the rim.

Park at Hemlock Creek Picnic Area to begin these trails. The picnic area is located off Dunham Road at the intersection of Tinkers Creek Road, at the west end of the reservation. The entrance road crosses over Hemlock Creek just north of where it flows into Tinkers Creek. The bridle trail begins at this point, near the bridge—a sign marks the start of the trail. (Look carefully, as the sign is somewhat obscured and off the side of the road).

Begin the bridle trail by fording Tinkers Creek to the south side. (This is not passable at high water: in that case, go back out to Dunham Road and cross, with caution, the narrow bridge over Tinkers Creek).

At the opposite bank, climb the short grassy slope onto the berm of Gorge Parkway. Follow the road to the left about 100 feet, then cross the road to where the trail is visible as it starts up a ridge. Climbing this ridge, the

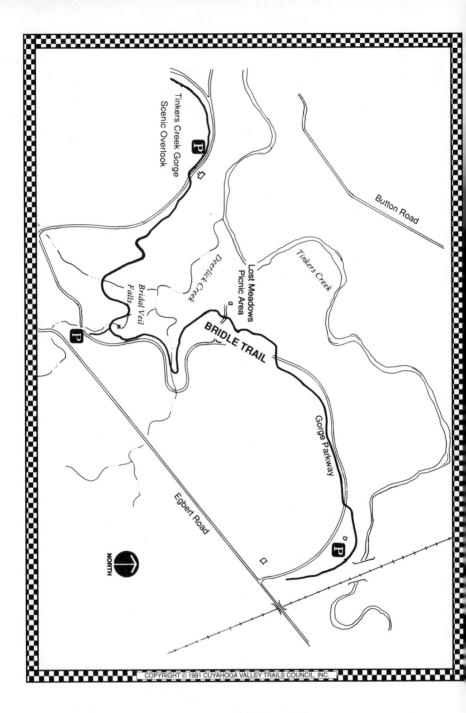

Bridle Trail — Bedford Reservation East

railroad trestle embankment can be seen to the right when the leaves are off the trees; the valley lies below and to the left.

At the top of this climb, keep towards the edge of the ridge, bearing away from the embankment, southwesterly. The trail sweeps around to the north to follow the curve of the ridge, crossing a side drainage, allowing beautiful views of the wide-spread valley when the trees are bare. Turn to the west and fairly soon you join up with the south rim trail and the Buckeye Trail.

Following this south rim trail to the right (south) you continue on the high ground, paralleling Overlook Lane, but out of sight of it, for about one mile until it intersects with Egbert Road. (The Buckeye Trail shares the route for most of the way except for a short section where it leaves the bridle trail.) Cross Egbert Road and continue south to Dunham Road, where this section ends.

Horseback riders wishing to continue to Brecksville Reservation can follow the bridle trail which leaves from Alexander Road Trailhead and follows Sagamore Creek to Canal Road. From Canal Road, follow the Towpath Trail through Pinery Narrows. At the time of this publication, the final connection to Brecksville Reservation was blocked at the Station Road bridge, however, there are plans to restore this historic bridge and open it to pedestrian, bicycle, and equestrian use. The future Station Road Trailhead will be located on the west side of the bridge.

Back in Bedford Reservation, if you take the rim trail to the left, you continue in a northerly direction through a scenic section along the steeply sloped gorge. Here the trail is again shared with the Buckeye Trail. Near Overlook Lane, bear to the east, leaving the Buckeye Trail, and cross Overlook Lane near the intersection with Gorge Parkway. Parallel the parkway, then cross it near the Tinkers Creek Scenic Gorge Overlook. Now on the north side of Gorge Parkway, rejoin the Buckeye Trail and move away from the road into a mature woods of oaks, hickories, and beeches.

About 1 mile from the overlook you come to Bridal Veil Falls on a tributary of Deerlick Creek. To the left is the falls overlook; the trail bears to the right crossing the creek by ford or footbridge. Steps to the right lead up to Gorge Parkway. The bridle trail and Buckeye Trail stay in the woods following the ravine of Deerlick Creek. Both skirt close to the road to get across to the other side of the ravine. This section is exceptionally beautiful, with hemlocks along the creek and waterfalls and rock tumbles below.

Cross the access road to Lost Meadows Picnic Area, go through another forested section, then cross Gorge Parkway. Here you follow along the south side of Gorge Parkway, with Shawnee Hills Golf Course to the right. Cross Gorge Parkway again, along with the Buckeye Trail, then cross the all purpose trail, and reenter the woods. The Egbert Picnic Area is to the right. This is the east end of the Bedford bridle trail.

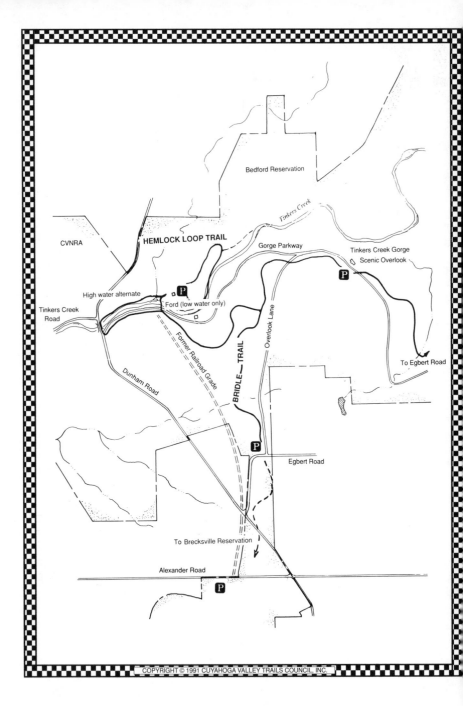

Bridle Trail — Bedford Reservation West

12

5.25 miles

Hiking time:

2 to 2.5 hours

Bicycling time:

45 minutes

Elevation change:

120 feet

Moderate

All Purpose Trail

This paved, 8 foot wide, multi-purpose trail offers access to Bedford Reservation's many attractions and is suitable for a variety of uses including bicycling, walking, and jogging. The surface is suitable for wheelchairs, however, some grades are relatively steep. Horses are not permitted on the all purpose trail, but a bridle trail parallels the route of this trail. A fitness trail is located along the all purpose trail near the Egbert Picnic Area.

There is easy access from this trail to two other natural attractions in Bedford Reservation: Tinkers Creek Gorge Scenic Overlook and Bridal Veil Falls. The trail crosses two major streams on bridges; the topography varies from level to hilly. Natural features along the way include hemlock ravines, oak-hickory forests, beech-maple forests, streams, and waterfalls.

You can park at the northeast end of the reservation at Egbert Picnic Area and at the south end at Alexander Road Trailhead. There are several other smaller parking areas along the way. At the south end, the all purpose trail links to the bike trail; continuing on the bike trail, you can go further south along the edge of CVNRA and beyond, to Kent, 28 miles away. Within Bedford Reservation, long loop hikes can be made by using the all purpose trail in one direction, and returning on the Buckeye Trail in the other direction. The all purpose trail is easy to follow as long as you just follow the paved surface. It stays mostly within sight of the park roads and is accessible from many points along the way.

Picnicking, grills, restrooms, water, and shelter are available at the major picnic areas. A Cleveland Metroparks Ranger Station is located at the east end of the reservation at the corner of Egbert Road and Gorge Parkway.

Starting from the east end, at Egbert Picnic Area, begin by paralleling Gorge Parkway on the north side of the

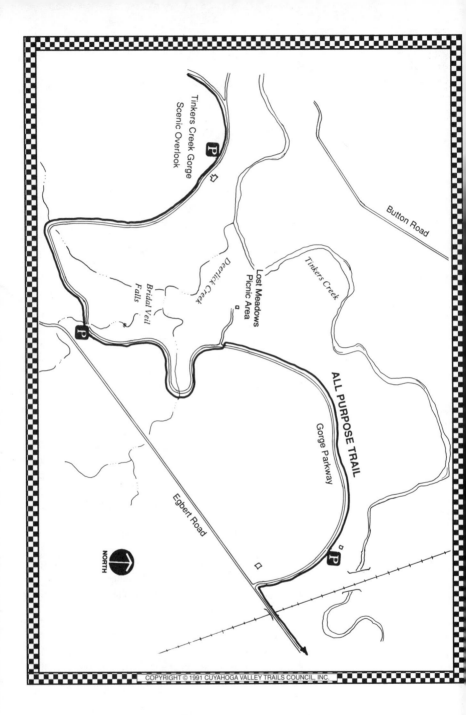

All Purpose Trail — Bedford Reservation East

road. Cross over to the south side before the entrance road to Lost Meadows Picnic Area. A side trip could be made down to Lost Meadows.

Continue along the south side of Gorge Parkway, crossing a bridge near Bridal Veil Falls. Here another 10 to 15 minute side trip (walking) takes you down the steps to view the falls.

The next major feature you reach is the Tinkers Creek Gorge Scenic Overlook. There is a small parking lot here near the observation platform. Just past the overlook, leave Gorge Parkway and turn south to follow along Overlook Lane. Cross Egbert Road, veer to the west to parallel the curving Egbert Road, then cross the bridle trail and descend towards the intersection of Egbert and Dunham Roads. Just short of Dunham road, you make another sharp turn to parallel Dunham Road on the north side.

At the next intersection, where Dunham Road crosses Alexander Road, there is a small trailhead parking lot. You can continue on the all purpose trail by crossing Dunham Road and paralleling Alexander Road for a short distance. You reach the terminus at the trailhead on Alexander Road.

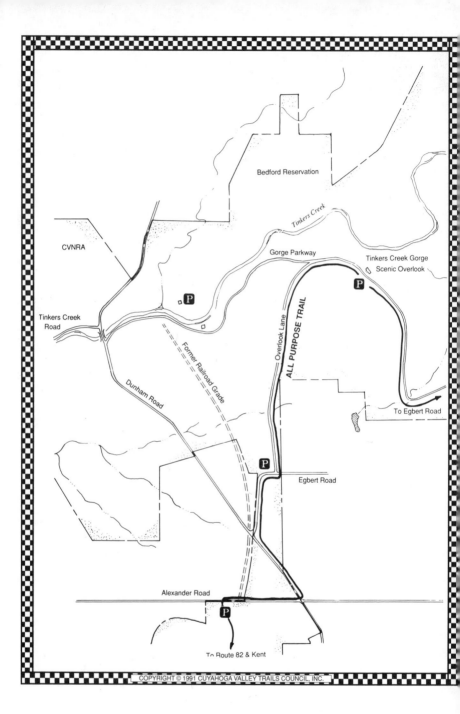

All Purpose Trail — Bedford Reservation West

13

9.8 miles

Bicycling time:

1.5 hours

Elevation change:

minimal

Easy

Bike & Hike Trail

Most of the combined Cleveland Metroparks bike trail and the Bike & Hike Trail in Metro Parks, Serving Summit County, runs just outside the boundary of the Cuyahoga Valley National Recreation Area along the east rim of the valley. Metro Parks, Serving Summit County, maintains a total of 23 miles of Bike & Hike Trail, including two southern legs which lead away from CVNRA to Kent and Stow. Only the 9.8 miles of bike path nearest CVNRA are described here, and we describe them as one continuous trail.

The beauty of this trail is that the entire length, except for one mile, is separated from road traffic, allowing you a quiet and safe ride on even the busiest of traffic days. The trail was one of the first "rails-to-trails" conversions in Ohio, utilizing abandoned railroad beds combined with utility rights-of-ways. Following the railroad routes, the trail takes you through some surprisingly remote areas, yet is never more than a mile or two from a crossroad.

Being separated from car traffic, the trail is ideal for family bike rides. For the most part, it is surfaced with compacted, crushed limestone, which works well for most bikes and is aesthetically pleasing. (Metro Parks, Serving Summit County has asphalt paving on the section that goes to Kent.) Grades are gentle, 3% or less. There is access to the trail at road crossings, where there is room to park several cars. Please do not block the gates: park vehicles need access for maintenance and emergency equipment. The best access points are noted on our trailhead map.

You can combine paved roads with the Bike & Hike Trail to make longer loop rides, avoiding retracing your route. Also, midway along the trail, there is a connector trail to the Towpath Trail, offering even more options for loop rides. Just remember, what goes down must come back up!

Bike & Hike Trail

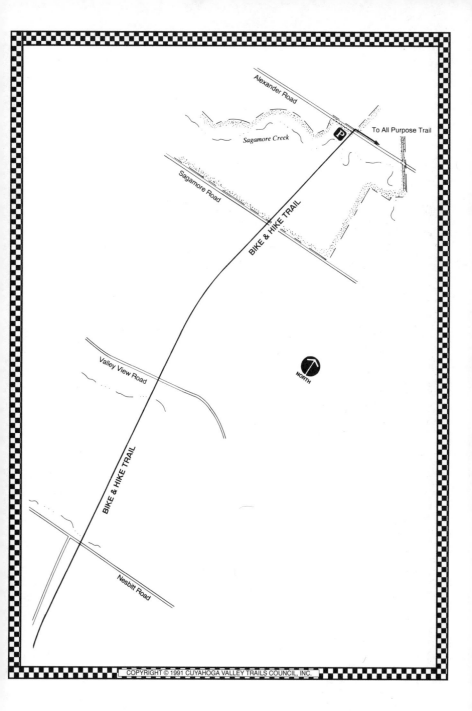

Bike & Hike Trail

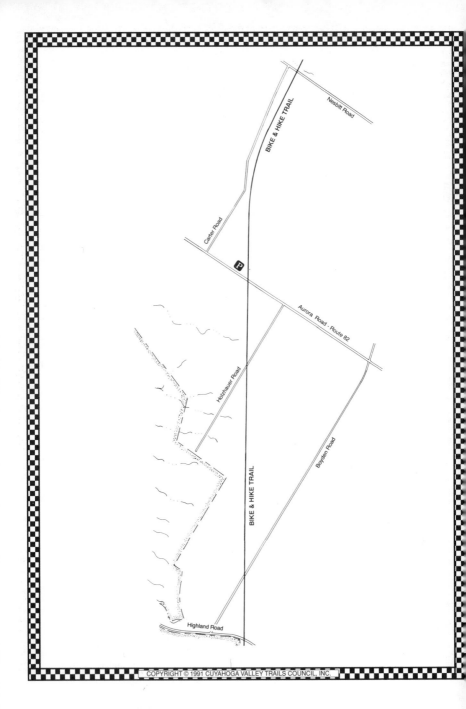

COPYRIGHT © 1991 CUYAHOGA VALLEY TRAILS COUNCIL, INC.

Bike & Hike Trail

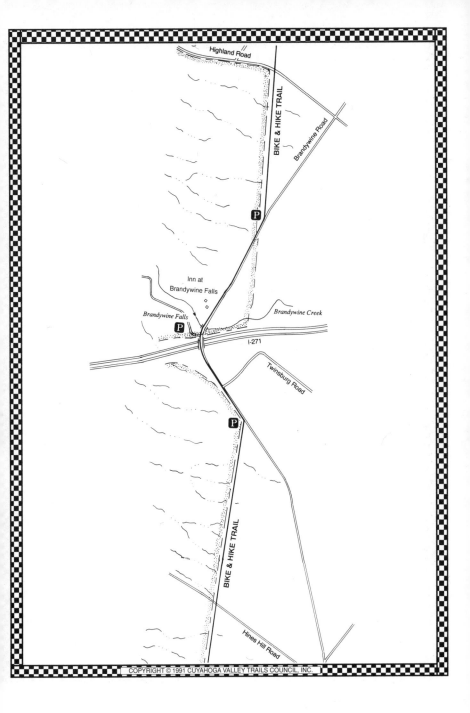

Bike & Hike Trail

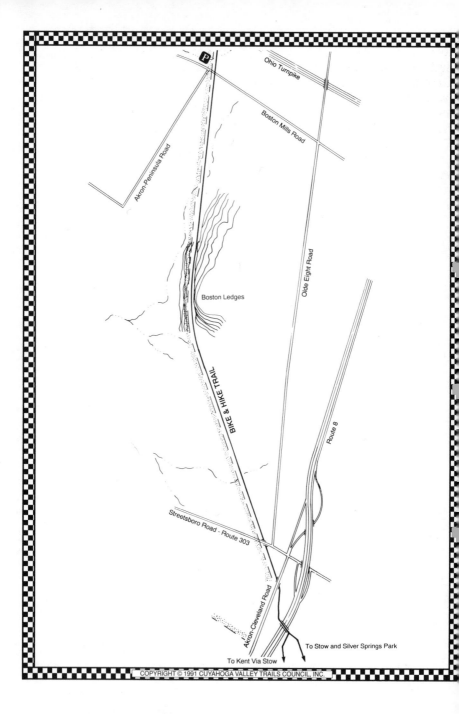

Bike & Hike Trail

The sections of the Bike & Hike Trail north of Route 8 follow the former route of the New York Central Railroad (originally the Pittsburgh and Lake Erie Railroad). Other sections south of the park follow the old "Alphabet Railroad"—the Akron, Bedford, & Cleveland Railroad that carried commuters from Akron to Public Square in Cleveland. That line merged with other electric railroads to form Northern Ohio Traction and Light Company, now known as Ohio Edison. The Bike & Hike Trail in Summit County, which opened in 1972, is the result of a cooperative effort between Ohio Edison and Metro Parks, Serving Summit County, with Metro Parks leasing the right-of-way and maintaining the trail. Cleveland Metroparks has developed the northern sections of trail in cooperation with Cleveland Electric Illuminating Company, where much of the trail runs under their transmission lines.

Woods, meadows, and some wetlands border the trail for its entire length. In the sunnier edges between the woods and the path, you can feast on wild berries in July and August. If you stop and look closely, in some areas you can find delicious wild strawberries in June, all the more delicious for their tiny size and the challenge in finding them. But watch out for poison ivy! It thrives along the edges. The ditches along the rights-of-way host cattails, and in some wet areas you can even find watercress. One of our largest summer wildflowers, the common mullein, thrives along the sunny borders of the trail. It is recognized by its flannel-textured leaves and yellow flowers and grows to 6 feet!

Your chances of seeing wildlife along the trail are good, especially in the early morning. Deer may cross in front of you, and keep your eyes out for rabbits and foxes. Birds feed along the shrub edges, along with colorful butterflies and dragonflies.

Starting at the north end, you can access the bike trail on Alexander Road, just west of Dunham Road, where you'll find a small parking lot. The Cleveland Metroparks Bedford all purpose trail also begins here, offering you a paved path heading north through Bedford Reservation. The bike trail starts off south, on a crushed limestone path, following the New York Central Railroad right-of-way.

The section between Sagamore Road and Route 82, 2.5 miles, is less scenic than the rest of the trail, as it goes beneath high-voltage electric transmission lines. But even in these areas, the surrounding vegetation provides pleasant scenery and wildlife habitat. At Route 82, there is room for parking several vehicles. Use caution when crossing this busy state highway.

The trail continues south on the railroad grade, and soon crosses Holzhauer Road. Here there is an option for a connection to the Towpath Trail, if you wish to plan a side trip or round trip. Follow Holzhauer Road south until it ends. Bear right onto the crushed stone path. This connector trail is a steep downhill, ending at the Towpath Trail. It uses a portion of the Old Carriage Trail, a hiking and cross-country ski trail. Note that bicycles are not permitted on the rest of the Old Carriage Trail.

If you do not take the option to the Towpath Trail, continue on the bike trail, following the railroad grade, to Boyden Road, then on to Highland Road, where there is space along the road to park a couple of cars. At Highland Road, you leave Cleveland Metroparks jurisdiction and enter Metro Parks, Serving Summit County. There are now milepost signs at each road crossing.

The next road intersection is Brandywine Road, where there is a small parking pull-off. Here the trail must leave the right-of-way and travel on Brandywine Road for one mile in order to cross I-271. Turn right onto the roadway to stay on the bike route. Midway along this mile stretch, you pass The Inn at Brandywine Falls, a lovely bed and breakfast in an historic farmhouse. The innkeepers are George and Katie Hoy (see appendix). Just beyond the inn is Stanford Road. You can leave the bike route here temporarily to reach the Brandywine Falls Trailhead, just around the corner on Stanford Road. The trailhead has restrooms and picnic tables, and is the start of the boardwalk leading to Brandywine Falls.

Back on Brandywine Road, continue on the Bike & Hike Trail route until you reach the sign directing you back onto the railroad grade. There is parking for about 2 or 3 cars here. In .8 mile you cross Hines Hill Road, then in the next section you cross the Ohio Turnpike on a bridge exclusively for the Bike & Hike Trail, just before reaching Boston Mills Road. Just to the west of the trail you can find an ample parking lot, the Bike & Hike Trailhead.

Continuing south, you finish the last 1.7 miles of trail through the most beautiful section of the old railroad cut. Here the trail passes between huge rocks, where the railroad was blasted through the Boston Ledges. Just north of the ledges, the railroad filled in a ravine to lessen the grade, and the sides slope steeply down towards the woods. There is private property on either side here, so please limit your exploring to the right-of-way itself. You can rest on a bench placed amidst the cool, fern-covered rocks, an especially welcome sight on a hot summer day.

Leaving this little oasis, you soon go under Route 303 and reach the ramp up to Akron Cleveland Road. There is a road from the trail to Akron Cleveland Road alongside the Bostonian Motel. There is no parking here, however, there is good parking at the next road crossing to the south, .75 miles away, at Barlow Road. South of the intersection of Route 303 and Akron Cleveland Road, the trail leaves the edge of CVNRA and soon splits into two legs, one ending in Stow and the other in Kent. Contact Metro Parks, Serving Summit County, for further information on those sections.

BRECKSVILLE RESERVATION

Brecksville Reservation is the largest reservation of Cleveland Metroparks, with 3090 acres of diverse parkland. It is located near the intersection of Route 82 and Route 21. The first parcels of land were acquired for Brecksville Reservation in 1920, just three years after the establishment of the Cleveland Metropolitan Park District. In 1921 the park board passed a resolution to create the 300-acre Harriet L. Keeler Memorial Woods. In 1935, during the Great Depression, a Civilian Conservation Corps camp was established in the reservation to construct trails and other facilities. It operated through 1937, when it then moved to Sand Run Reservation in Akron.

Chippewa Creek cuts a deep gorge through the north section of this reservation. Seven other ravines are formed by streams working their way to the Cuyahoga River. This makes for plenty of hills to climb and streams to cross when you explore Brecksville Reservation. The gorge area has steep cliffs, huge boulders, and cascading water. You will also find a variety of other natural habitats throughout the reservation, including oak-hickory forests, beech-maple forests, shady ravines, floodplains, and a restored tallgrass prairie.

At either end of this reservation, near the entrances, are several often overlooked, but fascinating, trees. Located near the corner of Route 21 and Valley Parkway, and again near the intersection of Chippewa Creek Drive and Riverview Road, are several dawn redwoods. These trees are often called living fossils because they thrived 100 million years ago in the age of dinosaurs. During the 1940s, they were discovered still growing in a remote valley in China. They have now been cultivated through seeds and cuttings.

These dawn redwoods are ancient relatives to our western giant sequoias (thus the Latin name Metasequoia glyptostroboides). They differ, however, by being deciduous, dropping their lacy leaves in autumn. You can recognize them by the pyramidal shape, horizontal branches, and grayish bark which is deeply fissured and reddish.

Brecksville Nature Center, one of the oldest buildings in the park district, is a good place to begin your visit to the reservation. Located on Chippewa Creek Drive, near the north entrance to Brecksville Reservation, the nature center is staffed by naturalists and has natural history exhibits. The building, built in 1939 as a WPA project, is constructed from American chestnut trees, killed by the chestnut blight in the 1920s and 30s, and from Berea sandstone quarried in the reservation.

Most of the trails in Brecksville Reservation radiate out from the nature center area. The trails include part of the Buckeye Trail, several hiking trails from .25 to 4 miles long, a paved all purpose trail, and bridle trails. Brecksville Reservation also offers golfing at the 18-hole Sleepy Hollow Golf Course. In the winter, there is cross-country skiing on the golf course and trails, and snowmobiling in an area along Chippewa Creek Drive when conditions permit.

A series of different colored markers designate the various hiking trails in Brecksville Reservation. Although they are well-marked, at times you will be following several trails and markers at once, which can be disconcerting until you are more oriented to the system. All color- coded trails, except the spur to My Mountain and the Buckeye Trail, follow a loop pattern, returning you to your starting point if you follow any one color marker. Considerably longer hikes can be made by connecting several of the loop trails. All the trails are described in the following pages except for the Buckeye Trail, which is described elsewhere with the other Buckeye Trail sections.

The main access to Brecksville Reservation is via Valley Parkway, off Route 21, 1.25 miles south of Route 82. A second entrance is Chippewa Creek Drive, off Route 82, just east of Route 21. Yet a third entrance is from Riverview Road; Chippewa Creek Drive intersects Riverview Road just south of Route 82.

14

4.5 miles

Hiking time:

2.5 to 3 hours

Bicycling time:

40 minutes

Elevation change:

410 feet

Easy to moderate

All Purpose Trail

The all purpose trail in Brecksville Reservation is a paved, multi-use trail. It has several access points and a northern and southern leg, and is suitable for cycling, running, or hiking. This trail gives you a wide variety of options and lengths. The northern split basically follows along Chippewa Creek Drive from the Chippewa Creek Trail parking area to Riverview Road. The southern split breaks off Chippewa Creek Drive near the vehicle ford across Chippewa Creek. It follows Valley Parkway to the western boundary of the reservation, at Route 21. Part of this trail includes a 1.4 mile physical fitness trail, located near the Chippewa Creek ford in the northeast corner of the reservation.

To begin from the north entrance into the reservation, start at the Chippewa Creek Gorge parking area, located just south of Route 82 on Chippewa Creek Drive. The paved path leaves from this parking area. As you begin, you pass the scenic overlook on the left, then the short spur to the Harriet Keeler Memorial on the right. Shortly past this, you pass the Harriet Keeler Memorial Picnic Area on the left, and access to Brecksville Nature Center and other trails to the right, across the road. Continue east along the road, going up and down several hills along the way, down to the floodplain of Chippewa Creek and the intersection with Valley Parkway. The Chippewa Picnic Area is on the right on the south side of the road. You can continue on the all purpose trail across Chippewa Creek, past a parking area and playfields, to finish at Riverview Road. It is here that you also find a physical fitness trail complete with exercise stations.

To take the southerly split (1.9 miles), return to the intersection of Chippewa Creek Drive and Valley Parkway. The trail heads southwest along Valley Parkway. Following the trail, you go past the Plateau Picnic Area then later cross the Buckeye Trail near the entrance to Oak Grove Picnic Area. Further along you intersect with the bridle trails and again with the Buckeye Trail as you approach the Deer Lick Cave area.

Cross Meadows Drive and continue along Valley Parkway; Sleepy Hollow Golf Course is to the north. You come to the end of the all purpose trail in Brecksville Reservation at Route 21.

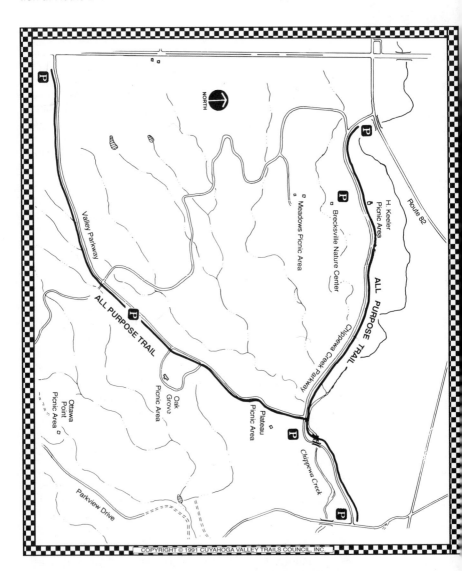

All Purpose Trail — Brecksville Reservation

15

🚶

2.5 miles

Hiking time: 1.5 hours

Elevation change:

220 feet

Easy to moderate

Chippewa Creek Trail

Chippewa Creek Trail follows the southern edge of the gorge formed by Chippewa Creek.   The creek has cut a remarkable gorge in the 12,000 years since the retreat of the last glaciers. Here the bedrock geology of the Cuyahoga Valley is easily visible, exposed in the cliffs of the gorge. Chippewa Falls, located under the Route 82 bridge, is formed as the creek falls over Berea Sandstone onto the more easily eroded Bedford Shale. The creek itself is littered with huge blocks of stone, eroded off the walls of the valley.

You can reach this green-marked trail from the paved parking lot on Chippewa Creek Drive just south of Route 82 . There are picnic tables near the parking lot and shelters along the way. The trail is described clockwise.

Follow the trail from the parking lot along the southern edge of the gorge. From the trail you can view beautiful hemlock ravines and large rocks deposited in Chippewa Creek. You also pass a large old oak on your left before reaching the Scenic Overlook Shelter and the intersection with the Scenic Overlook Trail (marked with white).

Bear left at the shelter, following the wooden fence. Scenic Overlook Trail (and later on, several unmarked trails) comes in from the right here. These connect back to a picnic area and Chippewa Creek Drive. Continue on the Chippewa Creek Trail through a hemlock woods. Hemlocks are evergreens of rocky, cool, shady areas. You can recognized them by their pyramid shape and flat needles with two white lines on the undersides.

In a little while, a shelter is visible through the woods to your right. You now begin a gradual descent along the edge of the gorge. The trail splits; take the right fork and continue downhill through tulip trees, oaks, and beeches. Continue this descent to the floodplain of Chippewa Creek. A marshy area is to the left.

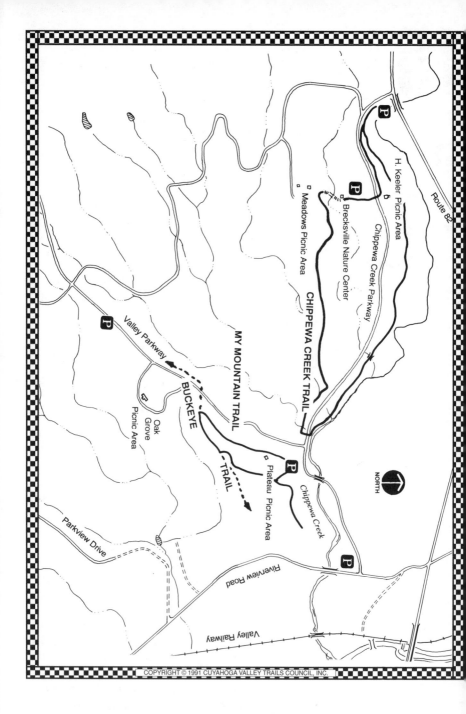

Chippewa Creek Trail and My Mountain Trail

Cross a stream on a wooden footbridge; Chippewa Creek is soon visible on the left. Cross another stream on a small wood suspension bridge. This was built by the 26th Engineering Company of the National Guard from Brookpark in April 1981. An open area provides another view of the creek.

You have reached Chippewa Creek Drive—cross the road towards Chippewa Creek Picnic Area. The trail now shares a return route with the Deer Lick Cave Trail (red) along the south side of the road as far as the nature center. Follow the trail as it turns to parallel Chippewa Creek Drive just south of the road. Cross a small stream on stepping stones, then climb out of the valley. A bridle trail splits off to the right, as you bear to the left, following the edge of the ridge with views of the stream below. The presence of cinnamon ferns and hemlocks hints at a cooler microclimate as you approach the cascade of the stream. The trail also passes some huge white and red oaks, and a number of sandstone slump blocks are visible below the cliffs.

The red and green-marked trails join, then leave, the bridle trail near Meadows Picnic Area. The combined trail leads to Brecksville Nature Center; follow this, then again follow the green-marked Chippewa Creek Trail as it goes away from the center on the main paved entrance walk. Cross the road where you will again come to Harriet Keeler Memorial Picnic Area. Turn left on paved all purpose trail. Pass the main entrance to the Scenic Overlook Trail, continuing of the all purpose trail. Turn right where the Chippewa Creek Trail and Scenic Overlook Trail leave the all purpose trail. Turn left along the gorge to finish the hike back to the parking lot off Route 82 where you began.

16

1.5 miles

Hiking time: 50

minutes

Elevation change:

100 feet

Easy

My Mountain Trail

My Mountain Trail climbs one of the many ridges in Brecksville Reservation, providing vistas of the beautiful surrounding hills and valleys. The deep forest and carpet of moss lends a feeling of a Tolkien fantasy to the experience. You half expect a troll or elf to appear from behind a tree!

The main access to this orange-marked trail is from Plateau Picnic Area, off Valley Parkway. There are parking, picnic facilities (including a shelter), and restrooms here.

To begin the trail from the parking lot, face the shelter and look for the row of large sycamores just to the right of the paved path. The orange markers on these trees mark the start of the trail. Begin by climbing a steep ridge paralleling the road. This levels out to a plateau. A woodland pond is to the left of the trail. There are fine old oaks and beeches in the woods, with an occasional hemlock. Off to the right is a nice vista of the next ridge; here you can get a sense of the rolling topography of the whole valley area.

To continue on My Mountain Trail, turn left where it joins the Buckeye Trail (blue blazes). (At this point you could follow the Buckeye Trail in the opposite direction to connect with the Deer Lick Cave Trail for a much longer hike.) Stay with the orange markers to continue on My Mountain. Again, there are beautiful views of the adjacent forested ridges.

My Mountain Trail soon splits from the Buckeye Trail—My Mountain going to the left. Close to the Plateau Picnic Area, a spur of the trail goes to the right to another ridge. Along the way you pass large white oaks and more scenic vistas, ending along a narrow ridge. A slump along this steep hillside has opened up a view to the north, and in winter, you can also see in the distance the Route 82 bridge over the Cuyahoga Valley. Return on the same spur to the main trail, then turn right and descend off the plateau towards the picnic area. Walk up the Plateau Picnic Area entrance drive to finish the hike.

17

Scenic Overlook Trail

.25 mile

Hiking time: 15

minutes

Elevation change:

20 feet

Easy

This short trail, marked with white markers, leads to an overlook of Chippewa Creek Gorge. You can start the trail at the Harriet Keeler Memorial (there is a small parking pull-off along the road). Begin by crossing Chippewa Creek Drive, then follow the white markers to reach the small overlook shelter. There are splendid views of the Chippewa Creek Gorge, a waterfall, and beautiful hemlock woods. From here you can enjoy a feeling of Canadian wilderness despite the proximity of civilization.

You can easily combine this trail with the green-marked Chippewa Creek Trail for a much longer hike.

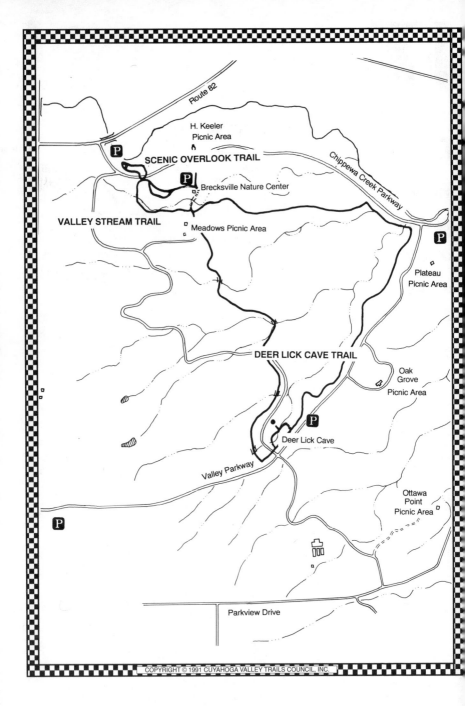

Scenic Overlook Trail, Deer Lick Cave Trail, and Valley Stream Trail

18

🚶

4 miles, hiking time

2.5 hours

Elevation change:

205 feet

Moderate to difficult

Deer Lick Cave Trail

This is one of the longer loop trails in Brecksville Reservation. It crosses several beautiful valleys, small streams, and high ridges, with the unusual sandstone formation of Deer Lick Cave being its major feature. This is a good choice for a long, rugged, and scenic hike.

Deer Lick Cave Trail begins at Brecksville Nature Center, where there are parking and toilets. (The nature center is located on Chippewa Creek Drive, about one-half mile south of Route 82.) Deer Lick Cave Trail can also be hiked from the southern end beginning at Deer Lick Cave itself. The trail is marked with red markers on the trees. It is described in a counterclockwise direction.

Begin Deer Lick Cave Trail at the nature center. Turn left as you face the center, passing the small amphitheatre outside the center. Descend through the forest, then cross the stream on a wooden bridge and take the steps to the left. (Valley Stream Trail, marked with yellow, branches off to the right before the steps). This section of trail is also shared with the green-marked Chippewa Creek Trail.

At the top of the steps, turn right. Skirt the edge of a pine planting as you come to Meadows Picnic Area. Cross a gravel road and the paved access road, turn right at the bridle trail, then left to descend to a stream valley. There is a spring, with signs of iron deposits, on the left. The trail crosses the stream on a footbridge next to the bridle trail ford. A very large white oak is on the left of the trail as you approach another ford and bridge; the trail then climbs out of this creek valley and skirts the edge of a large meadow.

When the trail splits just past the meadow, take the right fork, downhill. Continue down along the edge of the stream, then cross it on a bridge. There is an interesting shale formation where two streams converge near the bridge. The trail climbs out of this valley to Meadows Drive. Turn left at Meadows Drive to follow it 100 yards, then cross and enter a red pine planting.

The next small stream valley is also crossed via a bridge; in winter, this is a lovely sight seeing the trail curving down and around to cross the creek. Climbing from this valley, you can see Sleepy Hollow Golf Course to your right. The trail again drops to cross another stream. The Buckeye Trail now joins from the right (blazed in blue). Follow the red markers to the left as you approach Meadows Drive and cross it again (leaving the bridle trail). Thirty yards beyond the road, a branch of the Buckeye Trail goes straight ahead.

Take Deer Lick Cave Trail to the left, then descend stone steps to the sandstone formation for which the trail is named. Here you'll find lovely sandstone ledges, shelter caves, and waterfalls, with abundant mosses and large rocks. Cross the stream three times on footbridges to reach the main cave, on your left.

The main trail climbs out of this valley, paralleling Valley Parkway, while a short spur trail leads to the right and up to an overlook of the Deer Lick Cave area. Back on the main red-marked trail, you reach a kiosk telling the story of the Buckeye Trail, with mileages to each terminus in three directions. This is about the half-way point of the loop hike. You can find water and restrooms a little further on at the Oak Grove Picnic Area to the east, across Valley Parkway.

Deer Lick Cave Trail descends down wooden steps and crosses a stream on a bridge. My Mountain Trail (orange markers) and the Buckeye Trail go off to the right near here. Stay on Deer Lick Cave Trail, following the edge of the ridge, where you get good views of the surrounding woodlands to the left. Gradually you descend through beeches and tulips to reach Chippewa Creek Drive and Picnic Area.

At this point, the green-marked Chippewa Creek Trail shares the same return route west to the nature center. Follow both trails to the left, just south of Chippewa Creek Drive. After crossing the entrance drive to the picnic area, continue on the south side of the road about 200 yards. The trail continues into the woods at this point, then cross a small stream on stepping stones before beginning a climb out of the valley. The bridle trail splits off to the right, as you bear to the left, following the edge of the ridge, with views of the stream below. The presence of cinnamon ferns and hemlocks hints at a cooler microclimate as you approach the cascade of the stream. The trail also passes some huge white and red oaks, and a number of sandstone slump blocks are visible below the cliffs.

The red and green-marked trails join, then leave, the bridle trail near Meadows Picnic Area. Shortly after this, you retrace the trail you started on. Cross a boardwalk over a wash as the trail approaches the back side of the nature center. Descend steps to the right for the final stream crossing, then climb the hill to finish the trail in front of the center. Options here for longer hikes include going on to the Valley Stream Trail and the Tallgrass Prairie or crossing Chippewa Creek Drive to get onto the rest of the Chippewa Creek Trail.

19

.5 mile

Hiking time:

30 minutes

Elevation change:

50 feet

Easy

Valley Stream Trail

This short trail starts from Brecksville Nature Center and includes the all peoples trail, a paved interpretive trail. The short loop goes through several habitats: coniferous and deciduous woods, a tallgrass prairie, and stream ravine. There is parking for the nature center and trails on Chippewa Creek Drive; follow the paved trail to the center. Valley Stream Trail is marked with yellow hiker symbols on the trees.

From the nature center, follow the trail to the west of the center into a spruce planting. Adjacent is a splendid tallgrass prairie restoration project that has been developed by Senior Naturalist Karl Smith and his staff. An elevated deck with signs illustrating 31 prairie species is at the eastern edge of the planting. The trail continues along the south end of the prairie as you approach the Harriet Keeler Memorial area. On a large glacial erratic boulder a plaque reads "Harriet Keeler 1846-1921, Teacher-Educator-Citizen. She liveth as do the continuing generations of the woods she loved." The Scenic Overlook Trail (white markers) leads off to the right across the road, to Chippewa Creek Overlook area.

Valley Stream Trail goes off from the left of the memorial area. The ground cover here is myrtle. Descend on steps to the stream bed. Several large oaks are nearby and a wooden bench offers a peaceful place to rest. Cross the stream on a bridge, then climb back up the small ravine. Meadows Picnic Area can be seen in the distance.

The trail descends again to the stream and another bridge crossing and intersects with Deer Lick (red) and Chippewa Creek Gorge (green) Trails. Continue up the hill behind the nature center to finish the hike.

20

11 miles

Riding time: 2-3 hours

Hiking time: 4 hours

Elevation change:

260 feet

Moderate to difficult

Bridle Trails—Brecksville Reservation

The bridle trails in Brecksville Reservation wind 11 miles through some of the most scenic and remote areas in the reservation, through mature oak-hickory woods, across streams, and past meadows. The system consists of a large figure-eight loop with side connections out of the park to the east and west plus a small loop around the Brecksville Stables. The bridle trails are wide, well-graded, and paved with gravel. All along the way you can see Civilian Conservation Corps' fine stonework on culverts, bridge abutments, and retaining walls.

All trails can be reached from the stables, located on Meadows Drive off Valley Parkway. A concessionaire operates the stables, providing boarding and riding lessons but no rental horses. There is parking for cars and trailers at the stables.

The short loop behind the stable and the longer trails can all be reached by riding to the right of the stables along the pasture towards the woods, or to the left of the stables, just inside the woods. The short loop simply makes a circle around and behind the stable area, in the woods, and is mostly level. It skirts near private property on the west and south sides and goes through a beautiful planted spruce area.

To take the longer rides, start out on the trail to the left (east) of the stables. A trail from the stable drive leads into the woods and soon branches—the trail straight ahead goes around the stable; the trail to the left begins the longer trail. Follow this out to Meadows Drive, cross the drive and enter the woods. Here you are sharing the trail with the Buckeye Trail. The trail parallels Meadows Drive; a branch of the bridle trail joins on the left. Descend to cross a creek—Meadows Drive can be glimpsed to the left, crossing the creek on a arched sandstone bridge.

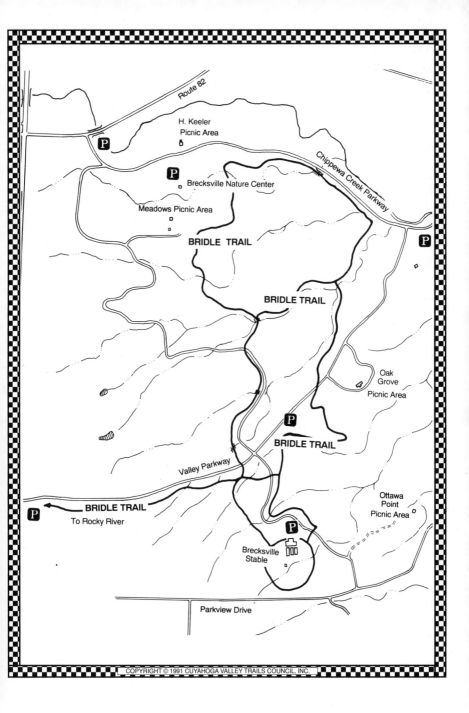

Bridle Trail — Brecksville Reservation

As the bridle trail approaches Valley Parkway, bear to the right to parallel the all purpose trail (paved) and the road. Here the Buckeye Trail leaves to cross the road. Staying on the bridle trail, swing away from the road into a woods of tall oaks and hickories. A large ravine opens out on the right. The trail follows this ravine edge around, then comes back out to the all purpose trail. Cross the all purpose trail, then the road, and intersect again with the Buckeye Trail on the far side of the road.

While the Buckeye Trail stays near the road, the bridle trail turns left and begins a steep descent into a beautiful, wide, creek valley. At the bottom, ford the creek and continue in the valley. The steep wooded hills to either side give a secluded feel to this lush, dished valley. It is in this bottom land that you come to an intersection: the outer loop of the bridle trail continues straight ahead in the valley, while to the left (west) a connector trail leads over to join the western side of the big loop. You can take this branch for a shorter loop ride back to the stables.

To continue on the longer loop, stay in the creek valley following the trail to the point where it joins the Deer Lick Cave and Chippewa Creek hiking trails (marked in red and green respectively). For a short way, all three trails share the same path. Bear to the left, cross a creek, then begin a gradual climb. The hiking trails split off to the left, while the bridle trail bears to the right. Cross another creek, this time on a bridge, go straight ahead, then wind out around a knoll and up onto a ridge. Another scenic creek valley is now on your left. Hemlock trees intermingled with tall oaks and hickories are especially attractive in the winter.

Follow the bridle trail down to the left, across the creek, then back up. Again the bridle trail meets up with the hiking trails, as all go out towards the fields at Meadows Picnic Area. To stay on the bridle trail, cross the field to the diagonally opposite corner.

At the far side of the field, enter the woods soon join the Deer Lick hiking trail again. The trail curves down into a ravine where you can cross the creeks via footbridges, or ford them if on horseback. Climb out of this valley; at the top you find the trail bordered by a ravine to the left and an extensive meadow on the right.

An unofficial trail takes off to the left; both the bridle and hiking route go to the right and take you back down to the creek bottom. Along the way the trail is edged by an old stone retaining wall. At the bottom you reach the intersection with the cut-across trail. It follows the creek downstream to the eastern side of the big loop.

The main loop of the bridle trail bears to the right and crosses a bridge; look to the right to see the rocky confluence of two branches of the creek. Climb out of this valley towards Meadows Drive. Turn left at Meadows Drive to follow it 100 yards, then cross. On the opposite side you go immediately into a planting of red pines.

Just beyond, the trail winds in graceful curves as it drops to cross a creek, then climbs again to within sight of Sleepy Hollow Golf Course. Beyond the golf course, as you approach Valley Parkway, you again cross the Buckeye Trail. Cross the parkway, then the all purpose trail and proceed ahead. In a short distance, you reach an intersection: the crossing trail is a bridle path leading to Route 21 to the west (where Valley Parkway extends west to connect with Mill Stream Run Reservation) and back across Meadows Drive to the east. Go straight ahead to return to the stables.

Before reaching the stables, you will come to another intersection where the loop behind the stables leaves to the right. Bear left to reach the parking lot. The loop behind the stables is short, level, and goes through an attractive fantasy-land spruce woods. It ends at the east end of the parking area, near Meadows Drive.

Stanford Trail

JAITE/BOSTON

The Jaite/Boston area is, in more ways than one, the heart of the 32,000 acre federal recreation area. Here public and private lands intertwine. All three park agencies have jurisdiction here-Cleveland Metroparks, Metro Parks, Serving Summit County, and the National Park Service. Private ownership includes two downhill ski areas and a water park/camping area.

The National Park Service headquarters is housed in the former company town of Jaite. Built from 1907 to 1924 to house millworkers who worked at the Jaite Paper Mill, the buildings have been adaptively restored for offices, meetings rooms, and the park's library. The parking lot across from the main headquarters building used by park staff during the week is ideal as an alternative trailhead for weekend trail users. A newly installed interpretive wayside exhibit, located on a small knoll just east of the railroad tracks, tells the story of Jaite.

Boston (later called Boston Mills), is a community that, during its heyday, was reported to be larger than Cleveland. Just north of Peninsula, it too was an ideal half-way point to overnight on the trip from Akron to Cleveland. It was from a boatyard in Boston that the *Allen Trimble* was launched on July 3, 1827, signalling the opening of the Ohio and Erie Canal. Nearly all the homes here are private, so please respect the rights of others.

Trails in the Jaite/Boston area have a little something for everyone who loves the outdoors: gorgeous hemlock ravines, waterfalls, mature forests, cool creekside bowers, steep ascents and descents, and opportunities to make longer loops by connecting the many trails.

21

3.25 miles

Skiing time 1.5 hours

Hiking time: 2.5 hours

Elevation change:

180 feet

Moderate to difficult

Old Carriage Trail

Winding stretches of trail which border deep, wooded ravines make up most of the length of the Old Carriage Trail. Along the way, three bridges, ranging in length from 150 to 166 feet, carry you across the side ravines. These features, along with vistas across the valley and invigorating steep sections of trail at either end, make this trail one of the most enjoyable and challenging for skiing or hiking.

The Old Carriage Trail is located on the eastern side of the valley in the area between Route 82 and Highland Road. This area has had a significant history in the Cuyahoga Valley, from the time of early Native Americans to the present. It is believed that Native Americans found the area suitable for encampments. After white settlers came, the high ground of Northfield Township was settled for farming, then, with the coming of the canal, rough roads led down to the canal boat loading areas. At one time, Holzhauer Road extended further south than it does now, connecting down the hill to a canal boat loading station at the foot of Red Lock Hill.

In the early 19th century, Wentworth G. Marshall and his wife Louise purchased 1000 acres of farmland in this area, bordered generally by Northfield Road, Holzhauer Road, and the canal. At that time Marshall was establishing himself in Cleveland as a drug store merchant. He bought an interest in a store on the site of the present Terminal Tower in 1876, then established a store at the corner of Superior and Public Square. He went on to create a successful chain of 46 Marshall Drug Stores. Marshall and his two sons all had beautiful homes built in the then just developing Shaker Village (Shaker Heights), but for the summers, W.G. Marshall moved his family to their summer home built on his farm called Rocky Run.

Both Wentworth and his son George enjoyed botany and invested much energy into developing an arboretum on the farm. They also planned and built carriage roads throughout the wooded acres, designing them to take

Old Carriage Trail

advantage of the ridgetops. Large culverts were placed in ravines and covered with fill to eliminate steep ups and downs. The Marshalls also donated a portion of the farm to Friendly Inn which ran a camp here for city youngsters.

After the Marshalls sold their farm, developers in Northfield began building an open-space development known as Greenwood Village. It was partially completed when it encountered financial troubles. During the early 1980s, a new owner decided to continue the development, however, in the meanwhile the remaining undeveloped acreage had been included within the boundary of the new Cuyahoga Valley National Recreation Area. Just in time, in 1983, the National Park Service purchased 518 acres and the builder went ahead with development outside the boundary of the park.

When the park acquired this property, it also acquired a ready-made trail, the old carriage roads which the Marshalls had built throughout their property. Much of the road system was still in excellent condition, however, in several places it was necessary to draw the park boundary across ravines, cutting off portions of the carriage road. This resulted in the necessity of building the beautiful steel box truss bridges that the trail is now known for! As you explore this lovely trail, keep an eye out for evidence of the earlier inhabitants, especially for the Marshalls who so loved and shared their Rocky Run Farm.

The Old Carriage Trail is a 3.75 mile loop off the Towpath Trail. To reach it from the south end, start at Red Lock Trailhead, located on Highland Road, .5 mile from Riverview Road, then go north on the Towpath Trail. From the north, get on the Towpath Trail at Station Road. A round trip from either trailhead is at least 5.3 miles. Please note that the Towpath Trail is a multi-use trail, but the Old Carriage Trail is reserved for hiking and skiing only, except for the southern portion which is designated as a multi-use connector between the Towpath and the Bike & Hike Trail. The Old Carriage Trail is described here from the southern entrance at Red Lock Trailhead. Red Lock Trailhead has parking and a portable toilet, but no water.

From Red Lock Trailhead, follow the Towpath Trail north. The old canal basin is on your right. This low lying area provides excellent habitat for wildlife. In the spring, you can hear spring peepers and toads, and wood ducks and great blue herons fly up ahead of you, usually spotting you before you see them. You can also watch for warblers, orioles, indigo buntings, woodpeckers, flycatchers and many other bird species as well as signs of deer and beaver activity.

Follow the Towpath Trail into a more wooded section, where the overarching trees create a tunnel effect. About .75 mile from the start, you reach the intersection of Towpath Trail and Old Carriage Trail. Turn right to follow Old Carriage Trail counter-clockwise. (You can also go straight ahead on the Towpath Trail for .5 mile to pick up the northern end of Old Carriage Trail if you wish to do the trail in the reverse direction.)

Turning to the right, cross the canal bed via a wooden bridge. A bench midway provides a pleasant spot to rest or observe. From this point, the trail picks up a

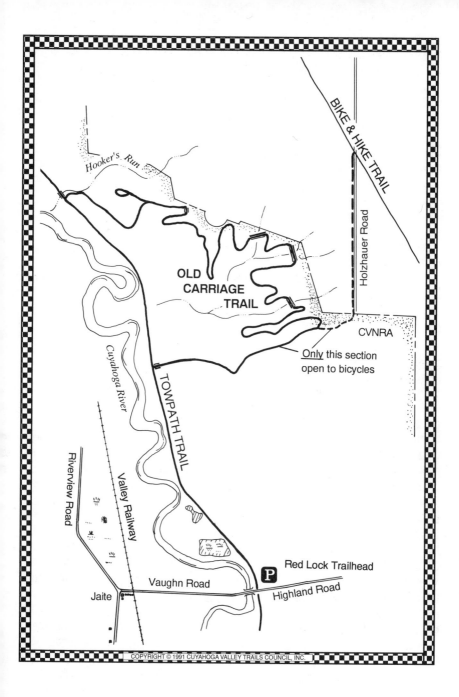

Old Carriage Trail

section of one of the old roads which is now surfaced for bicycle traffic as well as foot traffic; follow this for .6 mile to reach the top of the ridge, a gain in elevation of 150 feet. This section of trail is used as a multi-use connector to the Bike & Hike Trail. For a short span, you are on a narrow hogback with views to either side. At the top of the ridge you reach a trail intersection. Turn left to continue on the Old Carriage Trail. (The connector trail goes straight, ending at Holzhauer Road.)

Now begin a winding course along the fingers of land projecting between the ravines, following along the east rim of the Cuyahoga Valley. At 1.2 miles from the start of the Old Carriage Trail loop, descend to the first of three single-span steel bridges. From here you can see the small stream below rippling over a bed of shale.

After another half-mile of winding trail, you reach the second bridge, this one crossing a ravine lined with oaks, maples, and beeches. Two stately oaks at the north end give this bridge its nickname "Twin Oaks Bridge". You reach the third bridge, spanning a lovely hemlock ravine, shortly after this. As you can see from the way the bridges are nestled between the trees, the National Park Service required the use of special construction techniques to install them so that there was minimal disruption to the surrounding area.

Along this section, you are quite close to the eastern boundary of the national recreation area. You can see homes in the Greenwood Village development to your right. Please respect the private property, and if in doubt as to which way to go, bear to the left, away from the homes but staying on the high ridge.

Continue to follow Old Carriage Trail along the edges of ravines, moving away from the homes and out along a long narrow point of land. Continue generally north, then, on a switchback, descend to cross a short wooden bridge. Past this bridge, you once again come close to the park boundary, then reach the start of the 170-foot descent to the Towpath Trail. Just after you begin your descent, a short loop trail branches off to the right (for skiers this serves as an emergency runaway ramp!); this leads to a bench—perfect for lunch or quiet contemplation. Back on the main trail, it's all downhill from here!

At the bottom of the hill, rejoin the Towpath Trail. Turn left (south) to complete the loop. (Turn right if you want to add some mileage along the Towpath Trail). The canal is now on your left; the Cuyahoga River is to the right, at one point cutting in close to the trail. Just before you reach the point where you first left the Towpath, cross a bridge built upon the old abutments of a canal structure known as Goose Pond Weir.

Continue straight ahead to finish your ski or hike, unless you'd like to go around a second time! In .75 mile you reach the end of your tour at Red Lock Trailhead.

22

Stanford Trail and Brandywine Falls

1.5 miles

Hiking time: 1 hour

Elevation change:

190 feet

Moderate to difficult

Stanford Trail connects the Stanford House AYH Hostel to Brandywine Falls. Although relatively short, the trail has several steep sections, making it more challenging than it may first appear. Allow plenty of time for this trail, as there is much to discover. At the upper end are the gorge and falls of Brandywine Creek, midway is a short spur trail to a woodland pond, and nearly the entire trail is surrounded by a mature hardwood forest. Double the time allowed for this hike if you do not leave a car at Brandywine Falls.

There is also a short trail from the lower end of the hostel driveway to the Towpath Trail. From the Towpath Trail you can go north or south and make connections to other trails, including the Buckeye Trail, making Stanford House Hostel an excellent hub point from which to explore the valley.

The name of the hostel and trail derives from an early settler. In 1806 James Stanford arrived as part of a surveying crew from the Connecticut Land Company. He settled in the valley and became a prosperous farmer and community leader in Boston Township. His son George built the home which is now the Stanford House AYH Hostel. Descendents of these original settlers still live nearby.

Much of the land you cross on the Stanford Trail once belonged to Waldo L. Semon. He, a surveyor himself, became interested in the history of the area. He reported in a monograph that this area is transected by David Hudson's Trail, one of the earliest travel routes in this part of the valley. In 1799 David Hudson left Connecticut for the wilderness of Ohio, traveling mostly by water, as overland routes were plagued with difficulties. Going from Lake Ontario to Lake Erie, he eventually reached the mouth of the Cuyahoga River. Hudson traveled upstream until his way was blocked by shallow water and rapids. This "Hudson's Landing" is located near the confluence of Brandywine Creek and the river. From this point he set out over land to locate his Western Reserve holdings, an area which is now Hudson. He most likely followed Indian trails southeasterly towards the high ground in Hudson Township. This route became the earliest road in the area.

Stanford Trail was cleared by the Cleveland Hiking Club (CHC), which has since adopted this trail. Further improvements have been made by CHC, the Cuyahoga Valley Trails Council, and several Eagle Scouts.

This trail begins at the Stanford Trailhead located behind the Stanford House AYH Hostel. The hostel is on Stanford Road about .75 mile north of Boston Mills Road. You will find a small parking lot behind the barn for trail users and hostel guests. The trail ends at Brandywine Falls, a beautiful destination for lunch. There are picnic tables and restrooms at the Brandywine Falls end of the trail.

Start the Stanford Trail at the bulletin board at the northeast corner of the parking lot. Follow the mowed paths through the old pasture, towards Stanford Run. Just before the creek, a loop trail intersects to the right and left. Cross the creek on a bridge, then wind through the woods. Fairly soon, bear to the left to begin the climb up the hill. The trail was rerouted here to lessen the steepness of the climb. Some casual trails along the way have been blocked off by brush; be careful to keep to the main trail.

Partway up the hill the trail skirts around a small ravine, then later follows the edge of a larger ravine. Some of this route follows long established trails and even have some domestic flowers planted by former land owners. Cross the second ravine on a small wood bridge. Soon after this bridge you reach the historic David Hudson Trail. Turn to the left along the historic route for about 50 yards, then turn to the right. You can stay on the David Hudson Trail, going north, to follow a short spur trail to a woodland pond.

After leaving the David Hudson Trail, continue on the Stanford Trail descending towards another creek valley. A set of steps helps you down a steep slope just before a bridge across the creek. Here in the lowlands the trail may be a bit obscure. You cross an area between two small creeks, then cross the second creek on stepping stones.

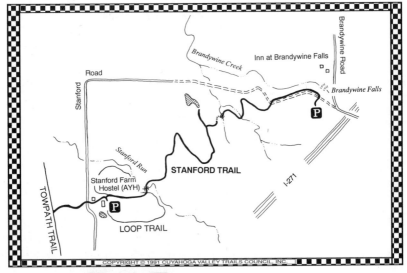

Stanford Trail

What comes down must go back up; you now leave the creek valley via a steep climb. From the older woods you come into younger growth and finally into a utility right-of-way. Cross the right-of-way and go onto Stanford Road. Walk along the road for about 200 yards until you reach the Brandywine Falls boardwalk. The scenic reward for your efforts lies just beyond.

The National Park Service has built a wonderful series of stairs and observation platforms to provide a close-up view of 65-foot Brandywine Falls. Hemlock, maple, and black locust trees surround the walkways, which are 7 feet wide and incorporate two major observation areas and benches along the way to the falls. The upper part of the boardwalk, the picnic area, and restrooms are accessible to those using wheelchairs.

The rimwalk (750 feet long) goes along the rim of the gorge to the remains of a grist mill. It is beautiful here in any season—in spring and summers the boardwalk is cooled and obscured by leafed-out trees; sugar maples light the gorge in gold and yellow in fall, and in winter, ice formations along the gorge are spectacular. At the end of the rimwalk, the short millwalk (50 feet long) continues past old mill foundations.

The ledgewalk (300 feet long), hugging the rock-walled ravine, leads to a lower observation deck where you might get showered by the mist if the water is running high. For good reason, the falls have become a favorite for artists and photographers as well as many a wedding party (permit required) looking for a romantic backdrop! Take your time to enjoy the sounds of cascading water and the spectacular views. If you are in the area in the latter part of May, you will be treated to the heavenly scent of the black locust trees in bloom. It's delightful!

On the north side of Brandywine Creek, is the Wallace farm, circa 1848, which is now The Inn at Brandywine Falls. This bed and breakfast, operated by George and Katie Hoy, is a delightful place to stay while exploring CVNRA. The Hoys lease the buildings from the National Park Service through the Historic Properties Lease Program. They have restored the farmhouse and barn and filled the rooms with 19th century style furnishings, many of them made in Ohio.

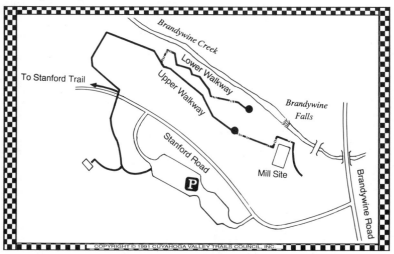

Brandywine Walkways

23

Blue Hen Falls Trail

1.2 miles (round trip)

Hiking time: 1 hour

Elevation change:

110 feet

Easy to moderate

The Blue Hen Falls Trail is one of the shortest trails in CVNRA, yet offers some beautiful scenery, including two lovely waterfalls. The falls are only a quarter mile or so apart, yet are quite different from each other. Blue Hen Falls is formed when the stream makes a clean 15-foot drop over erosion resistant Berea Sandstone to a layer of Bedford Shale. Downstream, at Buttermilk Falls, the stream cascades 20 feet over Bedford Shale.

Locate the trailhead from Riverview Road by turning west onto Boston Mills Road, just south of Boston Mills Ski Resort. Go one mile west of the intersection, past the Ohio National Guard buildings; watch for a sign and narrow drive to the right (north). At the end of a short gravel road is parking for 4 to 5 cars. A paved trail leaves from this parking area.

To follow the trail, start out on the paved path. The trail drops from the parking lot and winds down quickly to stream level. At higher water levels you can hear Spring Creek and the waterfall as you come down the hill and approach a bridge. Looking down from the bridge, you can clearly see the Berea Sandstone creek bottom, including fractures in the rock and a pothole formed by rock particles swirling around.

Just past the bridge, the Buckeye Trail (blue blazes) leaves the main trail on its way to Jaite and points north. Follow Blue Hen Falls Trail to the right until you reach the observation point.

From here you can see the capstone of sandstone at the head of the falls. This is the result of water eroding back into the shale on the wall of the falls, forming an undercut. At the base of the falls is a plunge pool, a large cavity formed from the force of falling water striking the Bedford Shale below. Mineral deposits under the falls seep from and discolor the surrounding rock. In winter, spectacular ice sculptures form along the falls. This is a favored spot for artists, photographers, or anyone enjoying the serenity of falling water in a woodland setting.

Continuing downstream, follow the narrow footpath, crossing the creek three times, to reach Buttermilk Falls. There are stepping stones, but in times of higher water be prepared to wade in water 6-8" deep. You can view Buttermilk Falls from the lip or from the bottom of the drop. Just before the stream drops over the lip, look for a wall of exposed rock dripping with moisture. Tiny plants, including liverworts, cling to this oozing rock, creating a miniature, emerald garden wall. The moisture from the falls also maintains a carpet of moss along the trail. Please stay on the trail to minimize damage to the area.

Return to the parking area via the same trail, or try some Buckeye Trail hiking as your time allows.

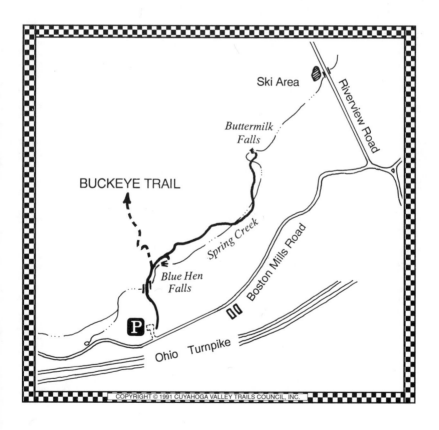

Blue Hen Falls Trail

FURNACE RUN METRO PARK

One of the oldest park areas in Summit County, Furnace Run is a unit owned and operated by Metro Parks, Serving Summit County. It is located in Richfield, south of the Ohio Turnpike Exit 11 and east and west of I-77. Most of the 889 acres were acquired in 1929 through the generous donation of the family of Charles Francis Brush, Jr. The Akron Metropolitan Park District developed the acreage into a park in the 1930s, employing work relief crews. The lake was enjoyed as a swimming area then, and more recently has been dredged and reopened for wildlife observation and ice skating. Owls, herons, warblers and waterfowl all benefit from the lake and surrounding habitat.

Two place names—Furnace Run and Bog Iron Pond—suggest a history of iron ore in this area. Bog iron is a hydrous iron oxide that was found in wet areas in Summit County. An early history of the area states that iron ore was discovered along Furnace Run valley and that there probably was an iron furnace in the area.

Two separate areas make up Furnace Run Metro Park. Reach the Brushwood Area via Cleveland Massillon Road (marked Route 21 north of I-77). Just south of the intersection with I-77, turn west onto Townsend Road. The entrance into the park is one mile down the road. The reservable shelter here, on the edge of Brushwood Lake, has been remodelled and expanded from its original use as a bathhouse. The shelter is enclosed, heated, fully accessible, and has a food service area and restrooms. (The restrooms remain open even when the shelter is locked). There are picnic tables, grills, and water along the playing field and along Furnace Run. Three easy trails are located in the Brushwood Area: Buttonwood, Old Mill, and Rock Creek Trails. All three can be intertwined to create a pleasant morning or afternoon hike.

Reach the H.S. Wagner area from Cleveland Massillon Road: less than .5 mile south of I-77, turn east onto Brush Road. This area and its one trail are named for Akron Metropolitan Park District's first director, who once owned the land and planted it with thousands of daffodils.

24

1 mile

Hiking time:

40-45 minutes

Elevation change:

minimal

Easy

Buttonwood Trail

Buttonwood Trail, in the Brushwood Area, is an easy, nearly level trail that makes a clockwise loop around a section of Furnace Run. It is named for the many sycamores, or "buttonwoods" along the way. Sycamores favor the rich bottomlands of rivers and streams and are most noticed for their mottled trunks with the patches of peeling bark. But it is their fruit, 1 inch balls hanging on drooping stalks, which gives them the nickname buttonwood.

Reach this trail from the parking lot by going past the shelter, across a bridge, and through a picnic grove. There you find the trail sign for all three Furnace Run trails. Buttonwood is marked with the pine tree symbol.

Start the Buttonwood Trail along with the Old Mill Trail; both lead off to the right. The woods here are mostly beech and maple, with the maples lighting the path with their brilliant yellow leaves in autumn. To your right is a marshy area along Furnace Run, a good place to watch for birds. Pass the point where the return loop of Old Mill Trail comes in from the left; Buttonwood Trail continues straight ahead. Shortly after this point is a good view of Brushwood Lake and some signs of beaver activity.

In about one-half mile, the trail splits; follow Buttonwood to the right, crossing Furnace Run on stepping stones. At this point you are about halfway and are going back upstream along Furnace Run. At several points, cross side creeks on stepping stones. It's along through here that the sycamores ("buttonwoods") dominate. Some are quite large and have grown into interesting shapes as they reach out over the water. End the trail near Brushwood Lake: cross the creek on a bridge, coming out into the mowed meadow near the shelter. The parking lot is just to the left.

25

1 mile

Hiking time:

40-45 minutes

Elevation change:

minimal

Easy

Old Mill Trail

Old Mill Trail, in the Brushwood Area of Furnace Run Metro Park, provides an easy walk along Furnace Run and the ridge above it. Woods of beech and maples surround the trail, with wildflowers at your feet in the spring and the sunshine of golden leaves overhead in the fall. The trail is marked with the Metro Parks symbol of a deer hoof print.

Begin Old Mill Trail from the parking lot of the Brushwood Area. Go past the shelter, across a bridge, and into the picnic grove. Turn to the right: Old Mill Trail and Buttonwood Trail start off together. Fairly soon, you come to the point where the return loop of Old Mill Trail comes in from the left; continue straight here, along with Buttonwood Trail.

In a half-mile, the two trails split: go to the left to stay on Old Mill Trail. Climb a short, steep rise to reach the ridge above. Years ago a severe storm downed a number of trees on this ridge; they now lie on the forest floor providing food and shelter to numerous insects, birds, and small mammals. Follow the ridge on this return side of the loop. You are traveling north, paralleling I-77. Three side ravines can be easily crossed via stepping stones or bridge.

Just before the trail descends to rejoin Buttonwood, you come to a 5 by 8-foot boulder commemorating the gentleman who formerly owned the land:

BRUSH WOOD
Is given in memory of
CHARLES FRANCIS BRUSH JUNIOR
To all those who love
As he loved
"The far sky and the smiling land"
1927

Complete the trail by descending the hill and turning right, back to your starting point in the picnic grove. You can continue onto Rock Creek Trail for a longer hike.

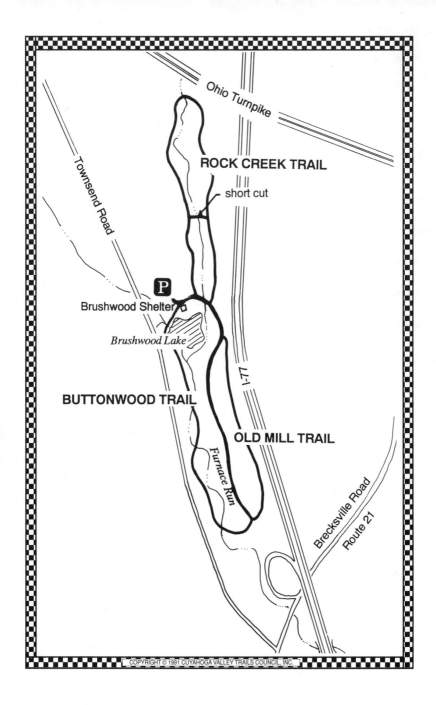

Buttonwood Trail, Old Mill Trail, and Rock Creek Trail

26

1.2 miles

Hiking time:

40-45 minutes

Elevation change:

minimal

Easy

Rock Creek Trail

Another easy trail in the Brushwood Area of Furnace Run Metro Park, Rock Creek Trail follows part of the course of a small tributary of Furnace Run. It's good for family hikes, even with small children, as they love to toddle along next to the creek. If they tire, you can take the shortcut; it is marked with a trail sign and cuts the distance in half. This floodplain area is also great for spring ephemeral wildflowers. Rock Creek Trail is marked with the Metro Parks oak leaf symbol and begins from the picnic grove along with two other trails.

Begin Rock Creek Trail by going across the playing field, past the shelter, over the creek, and into the picnic grove. A trail sign there directs you to turn left. As you begin Rock Creek Trail, you will likely hear the sounds from I-77, built since this area has been a park. But the creek here commands your attention, as you follow it upstream, crossing it and its many side creeks on sandstone stepping stones. Mature maples, beeches, and other deciduous trees line the trail. The shortcut trail, marked with a trail sign, leads across the creek and back to the playing field.

If you do the whole loop, about halfway around you cross the stream and change direction, now heading south. On the return side of the loop, you go through deciduous woods, then a stand of white pines. A lovely picnic area is situated along the creek. Leaving the picnic area, you pass Bog Iron Pond. This pond is slowly but surely losing its pond-ness and taking on the look of a marsh. It was probably dug sometime in the 19th century by bog iron miners for charcoal furnaces in the area.

Complete Rock Creek Trail by following the path out into the playfield above the shelter. The parking lot is directly ahead, beyond the border of trees.

27

🚶 ⛷️

1 mile

Hiking time:

30-45 minutes

Elevation change:

minimal

Easy

H. S. Wagner Daffodil Trail

And then my heart with pleasure fills,
And dances with the daffodils.

William Wordsworth

The Daffodil Trail is a favorite of many hikers of all ages, especially in the springtime. You may find yourself returning year after year to enjoy the welcome color of thousands of daffodils along the 1 mile trail. H.S. Wagner, the Metro Parks' first director, planted the flowers on this property which he had bought for a homesite. He never built here, and later sold the land to the Metro Parks, allowing it to be enjoyed by all.

The Daffodil Trail is located in the H.S. Wagner unit of Furnace Run Metro Park on Brush Road, about halfway between Black Road and Cleveland Massillon Road. You can reach Brush Road from Cleveland Massillon Road, south of where I-77 intersects or by taking Black Road north from Route 303. There is a small parking lot here but no other facilities.

Begin the Daffodil Trail at the parking lot. The trail starts off wide and level, with hardwoods to either side, passes a row of lovely hemlock trees, then opens out into a grassy area. A bench and a tall old oak tree invite you to rest awhile in this peaceful setting.

From the clearing, the trail begins to make a loop through a relatively level area bounded by two stream ravines. Keep going straight ahead to take the loop in a clockwise direction. Large oak trees and beeches line the ravine that is now visible to your left, while at your feet are the beginning of the many clusters of planted daffodils.

The tributary to your left empties into Furnace Run; the trail stays on the high ground above these streams. Where the trail begins to curve around, you may be able to glimpse Furnace Run in the wide valley below. This is about the half-way point; continuing on around you come to the other tributary valley which bounds this trail. Again, large, older trees line the trail and slopes, including some tall shagbark hickories, obvious by their loose, "shaggy" bark. The hickories, oaks, and beeches that you see through here are all indicative of a mature woods. The area to the right, however, has much younger trees, indicating the area was cleared in recent years.

To complete the loop, follow the path back into the grassy clearing. A couple of American holly trees stand out amongst the plants edging the grass. Bear to the left to follow the trail back to the parking lot.

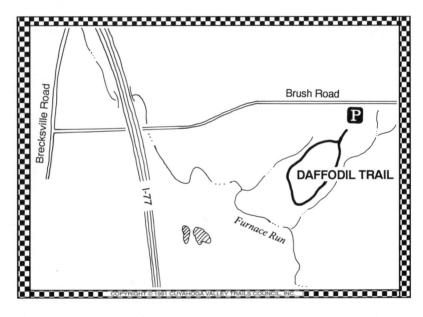

H. S. Wagner Daffodil Trail

28

Towpath Trail
Peninsula to Everett

3.1 miles

Hiking time: 2 hours

Elevation change:

minimal

Easy

The section of Towpath Trail from Peninsula to Everett travels through Deep Lock Quarry Metro Park and is used by the Buckeye Trail as it continues its 1200-mile loop of Ohio. The trail heads south out of Peninsula and, as in the northern section, is generally level and easy to follow.

Canal travelers moving at a steady three miles per hour found Peninsula a perfect place to break the journey. It is no wonder that hotels, bars, and other "recreation establishments" soon flourished. It is hard now to imagine this sleepy little village, an island of quiet surrounded on all sides by development and superhighways, was once the major hub of activity for miles around. A walk around town may pique your curiosity further. A visit to the Peninsula Library and Historical Society (on Riverview Road just south of Route 303) will reveal much of the area's history.

There is no public parking for the trail in Peninsula other than along Main Street. An alternative is to park at Deep Lock Quarry Metro Park. At the south end, park at the Everett Road Covered Bridge Trailhead on Everett Road.

Please take note: much of the Towpath Trail is under construction. As a hiker, jogger, bicyclist, or skier you will notice that some sections of the trail will be marked **"Closed, 8 a.m. to 5 p.m."**or **"Caution—under construction—hazardous conditions may exist."** Please heed these signs. As time goes on, more and more of the Towpath Trail will be complete and available for all to enjoy.

Access to the Towpath Trail in Peninsula is found just west of the Route 303 bridge over the Cuyahoga River. Follow the trail south by hopping the guard rail and scrambling down the short but steep embankment to the trail. To your right (west) and above you stands the historic Fox House (c. 1880). Faithfully restored by the

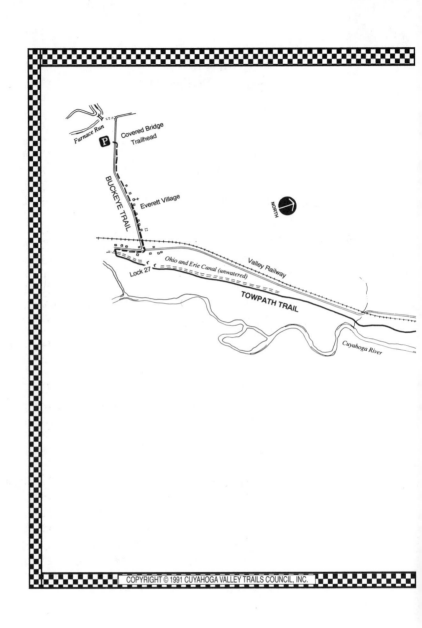

Towpath Trail — Peninsula to Everett

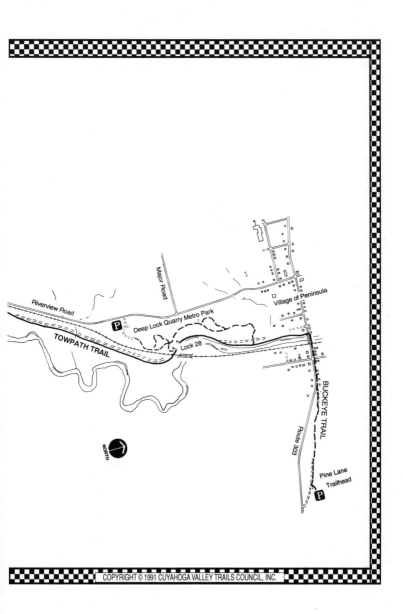

Major Road

Riverview Road

Deep Lock Quarry Metro Park

Village of Peninsula

TOWPATH TRAIL

Lock 28

NORTH

BUCKEYE TRAIL

Route 303

Pine Lane
Trailhead

National Park Service in 1985, this slate-roofed structure stands near the site of one of the Peninsula boat yards. The Fox House now serves as administrative offices for the Cuyahoga Valley Line excursion railroad.

Soon along this section you notice the distinct shape of the canal bed to the west (right). It is on the opposite side of where it was on the northern stretch. The towpath was always located between the canal and the river, serving two purposes. First, it acted as a dike to keep the canal out of the river, and the river out of the canal, and second, this location kept it away from the hillside and the potential of being blocked by mud slides. The switch occurred just north of Lock 29. Here the canal also crossed the Cuyahoga River on an aqueduct, similar to the aqueduct at Tinkers Creek, nearly 11 miles north.

Soon the trail takes you into Deep Lock Quarry Metro Park, operated by Metro Parks, Serving Summit County. A small footbridge to the west marks the northernmost extent of Metro Park's Towpath Trail. At mile 25, just over half a mile from Route 303, you find the magnificently preserved remains of Lock 28, or Deep Lock. At 17 feet, this lock had the largest drop of all the locks on the 308-mile long Ohio and Erie Canal. The usual drop on a lift lock was 8 to 12 feet. The additional depth apparently was not economical and the canal builders never repeated the experiment.

You may want to spend a moment at this lock. Of all the locks on the section of the Towpath Trail now open, this one is by far in the best condition. Note the holes in the top of the lock wall. These are locations of wooden mooring posts used to tie the boats off to the sides to prevent them from bumping about in the lock chamber during filling and draining. Other features, not visible in watered locks, are seen, such as the square openings in the lock walls used as culverts to move water from high to low level when the gates were closed.

Back on the trail, climb up and over the Valley Railway (which filled in the canal prism after 1913) and head south. The scenery here is a pleasant mix of farm fields, river, and floodplain. In winter you notice your closeness to Riverview Road, which parallels on the west (right), but summer's foliage hides all but the occasional sound of a car or bicyclist passing by. This stretch of towpath is broken in a number of areas by side washouts requiring a scramble into and out of the canal prism by various log or bridge crossings.

Here the agrarian setting in the valley is preserved. The rich bottom lands of the Cuyahoga River have been farmed for thousands of years, and the National Park Service has developed a leasing program to keep these fields farmed. Without it, these fields would slowly go into succession, losing an important page of the cultural history of settlement and development of the valley.

Near mile 27 stands, coincidentally, Lock 27! This marks your arrival at the community of Everett. Here the canal crossed Furnace Run, for which Furnace Run Metro

Park, far upstream, is named. Soon after the canal was finished in 1828, Furnace Run jumped its banks, deposited a load of silt into the canal, and blocked all boat passage. One of the boats was carrying cornmeal, so passengers and crew alike ate primarily johnnycakes for several days while crews cleaned out the canal. Lock 27 has been known as Johnnycake Lock ever since.

Follow the trail to the west (right) across the canal prism and out to Riverview Road. If your interests run to history or engineering, first follow the towpath to the creek. Here you see the remains of the stone abutments of the Furnace Run Aqueduct. In low water, you can see small iron pins built into the stone used to tie the iron work of the aqueduct to its supports.

Back on Riverview Road, you can see the remains of Everett Village. Up until the mid-1970s, the village had a small population and supported a gas station and general store. The National Park Service then purchased many of the structures, hoping to turn the area into an artist-in-residence community. However, after a number of disappointments, these plans were abandoned in favor of restoring the buildings for use as offices for CVNRA and allied organizations. Most of the buildings you see have been stabilized, protected by temporary metal roofs, and wait patiently to be returned to a period of usefulness.

Follow Everett Road one-half mile west to the Everett Road Covered Bridge Trailhead.

South of the village of Everett, the Towpath Trail dead-ends at a beaver marsh north of Ira Road. The remains of three other locks can be found within the boundary of the recreation area and deserve mention. Lock 26, or Pancake Lock, is found about .3 mile north of the intersection of Ira and Riverview Roads. The spillway and west walls of Locks 25 and 24 can be seen from Riverview Road, a mile or so south of Ira Road.

29

🚶

4.1 miles

Hiking time: 2 hours

Elevation change:

150 feet

Easy

Buckeye Trail
Pine Lane Trailhead (Peninsula) to Everett

This section of the Buckeye Trail in CVNRA allows you to leave the hills behind and enjoy an easy walk along the Ohio and Erie Canal towpath. (Note: for introduction to the Buckeye Trail, see page 28) Along or quite near the trail you can visit two canal towns, two canal locks, and a quarry in Deep Lock Quarry Metro Park. There is enough to explore along the way, especially if you are interested in canal history, to warrant allowing plenty of time for this hike.

To follow this section of Buckeye Trail, start at the Pine Lane Trailhead located off Route 303, .7 mile east of Peninsula. This section ends at the restored Everett Road Covered Bridge, a scenic spot for a picnic. There is ample parking at either end of the route. You must return along the same route or arrange to leave a car at the end of your hike.

To begin, look for the blue blazes directing you west out of the Pine Lane Trailhead parking lot and onto an old road (Pine Lane). Follow the road until it ends and the trail becomes a narrow path on a brick roadbed. This was an earlier roadbed of Route 303; you can still find remnants of the old guardrail.

At the bottom of this road you come out to join the present Route 303 and get a short tour of Peninsula. There is much to see in this small town. In 1974, the Department of the Interior designated the entire village a national historic district. Once a bustling canal town, Peninsula includes a number of historic homes and commercial buildings. If you walk about two blocks off the Buckeye Trail, up to Riverview Road, you pass several historic homes. Nearby on Riverview Road is the Peninsula Library and Historical Society which contains a good collection of local history. Here you can also enjoy the Mural of Transportation in the Cuyahoga Valley—a stone mural on the face of the library giving a unique bird's-eye view of the valley. There are also historic photographs displayed in some of the commercial establishments.

Back on the Buckeye Trail, follow the blue blazes on Route 303 across the Cuyahoga River to the west bank. Here watch carefully for where the trail crosses over the guardrail and drops down an embankment to get onto the remains of the Ohio and Erie Canal towpath. From this point, follow the Metro Park trail markers (a blue BT in a directional arrow), staying on the towpath until you reach Everett, about 3 miles south. (See Towpath Trail, page 105, for more detail on this area.)

The Buckeye Trail leaves the towpath just beyond Lock 27, Johnnycake Lock, and comes out alongside the NPS South District Ranger Station. Following the blazes, cross Riverview Road and walk along Everett Road about a half-mile to reach the end of this section at the Everett Road Covered Bridge. This is a restoration of a bridge that was first built in the 1870s. The original bridge was destroyed by flood in 1975; in 1986 the National Park Service replaced it using new timbers, but in a design true to the original construction.

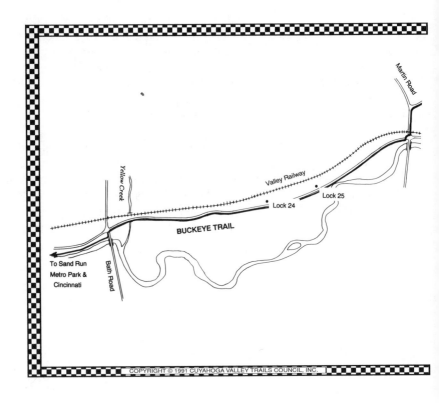

Buckeye Trail — Everett to Bath Road

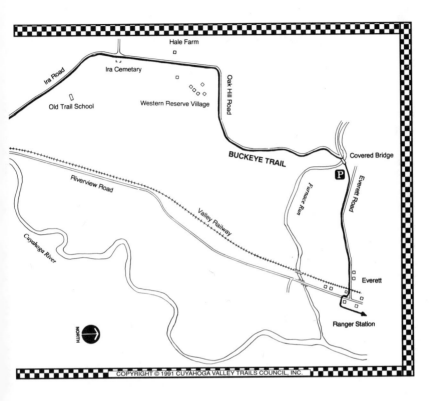

Hale Farm

Ira Road

Ira Cemetary

Old Trail School

Western Reserve Village

Oak Hill Road

BUCKEYE TRAIL

Covered Bridge

P

Everett Road

Furnace Run

Riverview Road

Valley Railway

Cuyahoga River

Everett

Ranger Station

NORTH

30

3.5 miles

Hiking time: 2 hours

Elevation change:

60 feet

Easy

Buckeye Trail
Everett to Bath Road

The Buckeye Trail from Everett to Bath Road is entirely along roads, but these are generally lightly traveled. Hale Farm and Village, operated by the Western Reserve Historical Society, is the prominent feature along the way. There is an entrance fee to tour the Hale Homestead and village. Your visit can include a tour of the homestead, one of the three earliest brick houses in this area, dating to 1826, plus tours of the other Western Reserve style buildings in the village. Craftsmen demonstrate skills used in the valley in the 1800s. The area also offers refreshments and a picnic area.

To follow the Buckeye Trail in this area, park at the Everett Road Covered Bridge, on Everett Road, .5 mile from Riverview Road. The southern terminus of this section is at Bath Road, where there is a small informal parking area.

To begin this section of Buckeye Trail, cross the covered bridge and turn left onto Oak Hill Road. This road winds through a very pretty rural residential area, then brings you into view of Hale Farm and Village.

Continue past the village to the intersection of Oak Hill and Ira Roads. The cemetery here contains graves of many of the early valley families. Follow Ira Road as it passes Old Trail School (an independent coeducational PK-8 school) and makes a turn to intersect with Riverview Road. Turn onto Riverview Road and continue south to the southern boundary of CVNRA at Bath Road.

Both the Ira Road and Bath Road intersections reveal very little of their 19th century settlements. There was a railroad station at Ira, named after a local landowner, Ira Hawkins. At one time there was also a cheese factory and a small book publishing company. Not far away, across the river, is the handsome home where the counterfeiter Jim Brown lived out his later years with his son.

The intersection at Bath Road used to be known as Botzum. Just before reaching the intersection, you cross over Yellow Creek near where it enters the Cuyahoga River. You can easily take a look at something here that few motorists ever see—the arched stone culvert through which the creek flows. From Ira to Bath Road, Riverview Road has been built upon the old canal, and all that is left to see are remnants of two locks.

At Bath Road the Buckeye Trail leaves CVNRA, beckoning you on. From here it continues south into Sand Run Metro Park and on around the state following canals, trails, and country roads. If you go on following the blue blazes, you will eventually return to this point!

Ledges Trail

HAPPY DAYS VISITOR CENTER AREA

Two trails are located in the immediate vicinity of Happy Days Visitor Center: Haskell Run Nature Trail, just to the south of the center, and Boston Run Trail, just to the north. Haskell Run Nature Trail is only a half-mile long but connects to the entire Ledges and Kendall Lake trails, giving you the opportunity to hike for a half-hour or all day.

Before starting on the trails, you may want to get better acquainted with the interesting history of the Happy Days building. Happy Days Visitor Center celebrated its 50th anniversary in 1989. It has not always been a visitor center but has served the public throughout its 50+ years. The area was a Civilian Conservation Corps camp during the 1930s when CCC was constructing trails and shelters in what was then Virginia Kendall Metropolitan Park. Happy Days was their last and largest building, built to house a summer camp for children from the Akron school system.

The name for the camp and building derives from the Roosevelt era "Happy Days Are Here Again" song. The building project itself was a joint venture between the Akron Metropolitan Park Board and the National Park Service, with the Park Service preparing the design and contract documents. Local money ran out before the project was completed, but the Metropolitan Park District's Director, H.S. Wagner, convinced the National Park Service to fund its completion. Little did the NPS know at that time that their efforts would be returned (many times over) forty years later.

Happy Days Camp continued here until the mid 1940s. From then until 1976, the Akron Metropolitan Park District operated the building as a reservable shelter. In 1974 President Gerald Ford signed the law to create Cuyahoga Valley National Recreation Area. A few years later the management of Virginia Kendall Park was transferred to the new National Recreation Area. Following this, improvements were made to allow for year-round use, and in 1980, Happy Days became the first visitor center in CVNRA.

The building is constructed of wormy chestnut wood and locally quarried sandstone. The many chestnut trees that had thrived in the surrounding forests were all killed in the fungal blight during the 1920s. Ironically, though the trees were killed, they provided an excellent building material, for the wood has exceptional workability, resistance to decay, and a desired rustic appearance. Therefore, all the CCC buildings in Virginia Kendall were built of chestnut wood, including the outhouses! In this way, the chestnut trees live on.

Inside Happy Days Visitor Center, you can visit the Great Hall which used to house the school children; be sure to look up at the partial second story. Here the counselors could peek down upon the children in the dormitory.

Happy Days is located on Route 303, between Route 8 and Akron Peninsula Road. There are picnic tables near the visitor center and restrooms and water inside. Inside the visitor center, you will find rangers who can give you information on trails and on the ranger-led programs, displays, and an introductory slide show. There is also a good selection of field guides and other books pertaining to the Cuyahoga Valley and the National Park System. The visitor center is open daily, 8 a.m. to 5 p.m.; closed on Thanksgiving, Christmas, and New Year's.

31

🚶

.5 mile

Hiking time: 30

minutes

Elevation change:

70 feet

Easy

Haskell Run Self-Guiding Nature Trail

Haskell Run Nature Trail is a short footpath that guides you through a wooded ravine, typical of many such ravines in the Cuyahoga Valley. It is an excellent introduction to this particular habitat in the valley, and so was chosen to be the first in a planned series of self-guided trails. For fuller enjoyment of this trail, ask in Happy Days Visitor Center for the self-guiding booklet which gives detailed information about the ravine habitat.

The trail is located just outside Happy Days Visitor Center and makes a short loop beginning and ending near the center. Happy Days is located on Route 303, between Route 8 and Akron Peninsula Road. There are picnic tables near the visitor center and restrooms and water inside.

Begin the Haskell Run Trail at the trailhead bulletin board just behind the visitor center, at the corner of the parking lot. This first part of the trail is perched on a narrow corridor of land between the edge of the ravine and the Mater Dolorsa cemetery. This is a privately owned and maintained cemetery, but you are welcome to visit.

At the junction with a service road, turn to the right, onto the service road, and follow it down into the ravine, then downstream along Haskell Run. Water is the most prominent feature here. While oaks grow up on the drier ridgetop, down here the water-loving plants, such as mosses, skunk cabbages, and sycamores, thrive. Especially in summer, you can notice the drop in temperature and increase in humidity in this well-shaded valley. In the spring, it's a wildflower garden.

Cross the creek on a bridge; just after this crossing is the intersection with a short trail connecting Haskell Run Trail to the Ledges Trail. Stay down by the creek to continue along Haskell Run Trail. This stream runs year-round and descends 360 feet in 2 miles, emptying into the Cuyahoga

River. The surrounding habitat supports a diversity of animals including frogs, salamanders, songbirds, mice, chipmunks, and squirrels.

After crossing the creek again, climb back out of the ravine. The trail brings you out at the west end of the large playing field. Crossing the field brings you back to the visitor center.

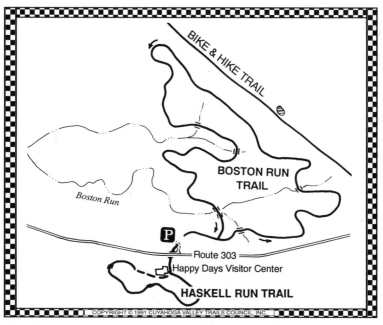

Haskell Run Trail and Boston Run Trail

32

3.4 miles

Skiing time:

1.5 hours

Hiking time: 2 hours

Elevation change:

80 feet

Moderate

Boston Run Trail

The Boston Run Trail follows the upper portion of Boston Run and its tributaries. It is mostly in wooded areas, with some parts crossing fields which are reverting to woodland. Stands of beech trees with their ghostly silver-grey bark and a rocky hemlock ravine add special beauty fo this route.

The trail's length and several moderate hills make it a good one for skiers of intermediate levels. Take extra caution here if the snow cover is marginal or icy—the hills are short and relatively steep. A good snowplow maneuver is advisable. When in doubt, sit it out!

The Boston Run Trail was originally established by the Akron Metropolitan Park District as a motorized vehicle trail in 1972. The trail remained open until the Park District transferred the entire Virginia Kendall Park area to the National Park Service as part of the new Cuyahoga Valley National Recreation Area in 1978. The trail was unused for several years until the National Park Service improved it, rerouted some sections, and reopened it as a cross-country ski trail.

To reach this trail, park at the Happy Days Visitor Center lot on Route 303, less than one mile west of Route 8.

Begin Boston Run Trail at the northeast corner of Happy Days parking lot, near the trailhead bulletin board. The trail is marked in a counterclockwise direction for the pleasure and safety of skiers, taking best advantage of the terrain. Follow the edge of the playing field; go past the exit of the loop trail to find the start of the trail. The trail veers to the left into the woods to begin the loop.

Very soon, begin a curving downhill run, then cross a bridge, and climb alongside Route 303. At the top of this hill the trail winds away from the road through a quiet woodland. There is another short descent, then a section now heading well away from the road through a beech woods, a wet area, and open meadows.

Your next downhill is a lovely curving descent that turns sharply at the bottom to cross a bridge over a branch of Boston Run. After the climb back up, you have over 1.5 miles of level to gently rolling terrain. If skiing, this is one of the most enjoyable parts of this trail, as you double-pole at a nice pace through a mature beech forest. Follow the trail along a hemlock ravine, then back into the hardwoods again, coming out along another ravine edge; the creek below flows to the main channel of Boston Run.

About 2.8 miles along the way, you come to a bench on your right, followed by two more benches around the bend. These are on a plateau between Boston Run and a tributary. On the left are aspen and dogwood trees, indicating an early stage of forest growth. The ravines have mature beeches and maples. This is a great spot to sit quietly for a bit of wildlife watching. If you are lucky you may see many birds (especially woodpeckers), small mammals, and perhaps a deer or two.

Meander on this plateau for awhile, then descend steeply into the valley of Boston Run one last time. Cross two bridges, then climb very steeply back to the playing field where you began. Turn to the right to return to the parking lot.

Ledges Overlook

THE LEDGES

For many years people have been attracted to the Ritchie Ledges area for its unique natural beauty reminiscent of faraway places. The dramatic rise of rock comes as a surprise to someone new to the area. The exposed rock, the graceful hemlocks, the cool water oozing from cracks in the rocks, and the mosses and ferns all seem more like the north woods or the mountains. This is understandable, because this habitat we enjoy today is related to the colder climate following the last retreat of the glaciers.

There are three hiking trails in this area, totalling about 5 miles. You can make connections to other trails in the area to lengthen your hike. The scenery, along with many picnic sites, reservable shelters, and large playing field make this a popular picnicking spot.

The Ledges, Pine Grove, and Forest Point trails are all part of the Virginia Kendall Unit of Cuyahoga Valley National Recreation Area. This area was Hayward Kendall's country retreat in the early part of this century. Kendall willed 420 acres to the State of Ohio for park purposes and the park was named in memory of his mother. Virginia Kendall Park was managed by the Akron Metropolitan Park District until transfer to the National Park Service in January 1978, it then becoming the first federal unit of Cuyahoga Valley National Recreation Area.

The Civilian Conservation Corps (CCC) built all the structures in the park in the 1930s. These include the Ledges Shelter, the Octagon Shelter (both reservable), the Lake Shelter, the stone steps to Ice Box Cave, restrooms, benches, and some roads and trails. The CCC also planted many of the trees and shrubs that you now find in the area. Part of the pleasure of these trails is discovering these reminders of the long history of this park.

The entrance to the area is reached by going south out of Peninsula on Akron Peninsula Road, then east on Truxell Road for about 2.25 miles. You can also reach Truxell Road from Akron Cleveland Road, .75 mile south of Route 303.

33

![hiker icon]

2.2 miles

Hiking time: 1.5 hours

Elevation change:

105 feet

Moderate

Ledges Trail

The Ledges Trail makes a loop around the Ritchie Ledges, starting out on the top of the rock formation. The ledges are splendid rock outcrops of a formation called Sharon Conglomerate. About 300 million years ago, a large, shallow sea covered this area. The Sharon Conglomerate was formed when fast-moving streams from the north carried sediment into the sea. In time the sediment was compacted into conglomerate rock comprised of cemented sand and small quartz pebbles, rounded and smoothed by the action of the water.

This rock resists erosion and is often found exposed where other materials have eroded away. It usually occurs as the cap rock at 1150 to 1300 feet elevation. That is the case here, where all around this hard rock the forces of erosion have sculpted a horseshoe-shaped island of land. You can also find Sharon Conglomerate rock cliffs at Gorge Metropolitan Park in Cuyahoga Falls, Nelson-Kennedy Ledges in Portage County, and in Jackson County 150 miles south of here.

A moist, cool microclimate along the ledges encourages the growth of plants which are typical of more northern climes. You can find ferns, starflower, hemlocks (evergreens whose needles are flat with two white lines beneath), and yellow birch trees along the trail. The birches wind their roots over the rock, clinging to whatever they can. Recognize them by their yellowish, peeling bark. The birds you are likely to see include woodpeckers, warblers, wood thrushes, wrens, and even the brilliantly colored scarlet tanagers. They all disappear quickly into the thick woods at your approach, so walk slowly and sit often to enjoy their winged beauty.

Begin the Ledges Trail at the trailhead bulletin board near the Ledges Shelter. Follow the service road north alongside the shelter. All along this road, small trails lead off to picnic tables scattered throughout the woods. At the first true trail intersection, marked with a trail sign, turn to the right. Soon there is a noticeable change in the woods, from oaks and hickories to hemlocks, and at this point you begin to see the fissured conglomerate.

Follow the trail as it drops alongside the ledges, where you soon reach the circular Ledges Trail. You can walk it in either direction—it is described in a counterclockwise direction. Turn to the left; in about 100 yards is Ice Box Cave. This narrow slit in the rock reaches 50 feet into the dark dampness. A spring seeps from the rock near a wood bridge just beyond Ice Box Cave. The temperature is noticeably cooler here, and a fern garden thrives on the rock above it.

Leaving the cave area, cross a seep on a bridge, climb the steps, and continue on. Informal trails off to the left go back into the ledges.

Continue on for a quarter of a mile to a bench and a set of stone steps. These steps lead back up to the playing field and picnic area. The graceful, curving steps were built by the Civilian Conservation Corps from Berea Sandstone quarried from Deep Lock Quarry. Just beyond the steps a trail to the right connects with the Haskell Run Trail and Happy Days Visitor Center. Staying on the Ledges Trail, take the boardwalks and steps around the nose of exposed rock. A trail to the left leads back up to the Ledges Shelter, and shortly after this a trail to the right goes to the Octagon Shelter. Stay at the base of the rock if you wish to complete the loop.

Continue along the base of the towering rock face for about .5 mile. The ledges begin to diminish towards the southern point of the loop. At the trail intersection turn to the left and climb the hill. The trail to the right leads to the Lake Shelter, .9 miles away.

When you reach the top of the rock again, watch for side trails leading west towards the edge of the ledges. Follow one of these to find the exposed rock overlook where you can enjoy an expansive view of the Cuyahoga Valley. Past the overlook, skirt the edge of the field, just inside the woods, then cross the entrance drive. After a short walk through deciduous trees, you reach a wood bridge. Across the bridge is a feathery, fairylike forest of hemlocks. Complete the loop trail just before Ice Box Cave; watch for the trail leading up to the left to take you to the top of the ledges, then another left that leads back to the shelter. All around the edges of the field, trails lead to picturesque picnic sites where you can get close looks at the cracks and fissures in the rock.

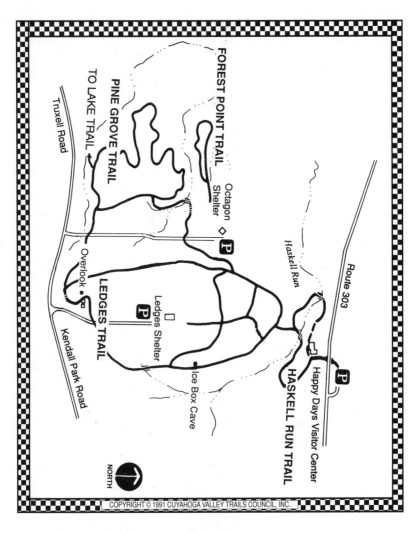

FOREST POINT TRAIL

PINE GROVE TRAIL

TO LAKE TRAIL

Truxell Road

Octagon
Shelter

◇

P

Overlook

LEDGES TRAIL

P Ledges Shelter

Kendall Park Road

Ice Box Cave

Haskell Run

Route 303

Happy Days Visitor Center

HASKELL RUN TRAIL

P

NORTH

Ledges Area

34

Pine Grove Trail

2.2 miles

Hiking time:

1.25 hours

Elevation change:

100 feet

Easy

The Pine Grove Trail circles through the forests west of the Ritchie Ledges in the Virginia Kendall unit of CVNRA. It is named after the red pine plantation through which it passes. This trail can be combined with others in the Ledges and Kendall Lake areas for longer hikes. Near the start of the trail is the Octagon Shelter, a CCC era structure, which can be reserved through CVNRA (see appendix). Picnic sites with grills line the edges of the playing field near the shelter, and restrooms and water (shut off in winter) are nearby.

This trail starts from the Octagon Shelter; to reach it, go south of Peninsula on Akron Peninsula Road to Truxell Road and turn left. The entrance drive to the Octagon is about 2 miles down Truxell Road.

Begin Pine Grove Trail at the trailhead bulletin board located at the upper, southeast corner of the Octagon parking lot. The first half mile or so is an access trail to the main loop. Follow this south, cross the entrance drive, and continue into the woods. You come to a wooden staircase which leads down into a beech and maple ravine. After crossing the creek three times, climb another set of steps to reach the Pine Grove Trail loop.

From here, the Pine Grove Trail can be followed in either direction. To follow the trail counterclockwise, turn to the right; the trail heads north along a ravine. Wind along several small ravines until you come to the red pines for which the trail is named. Pines were often planted in plantations such as this during the reforestation efforts of the 1930s.

Past the pines and about one mile from the start of the trail, you come to a trail leading off to the right towards Camp Butler. Follow Pine Grove beyond this intersection; it drops partway into a beech ravine, then leaves the beeches to reenter the pines again. About 3/4 of the way around the loop, a trail from the Kendall Lake area comes in from the right. Continuing on around, at the next trail intersection bear to the left; the trail straight ahead leads up to the south end of the ledges.

An aspen grove borders the pine woods along this portion of the trail. Aspens do well on cut-over areas and probably established themselves here after the area was left to reforest. Soon you have completed the loop; take the trail to the right back across the creek and up the stairs to return to the Octagon Trailhead.

35

.5 mile

Hiking time:

30 minutes

Elevation change:

minimal

Easy

Forest Point Trail

This short, easy trail begins at the southwest corner of the playing field behind the Octagon Shelter. It provides a pleasant walk for people of all ages—perfect for after a holiday picnic!

To reach Octagon Shelter, go south of Peninsula on Akron Peninsula Road to Truxell Road and turn left. The entrance drive to Octagon Shelter is about 2 miles down Truxell Road.

Little description is needed for following the trail: shortly after entering the woods, the trail splits to the right and left. Follow it in either direction to go out to a point of land overlooking Ritchie Run.

The forest here is typical of deciduous woods of Cuyahoga Valley National Recreation Area. One of the more interesting trees is the beech. The smooth, light grey bark of these large trees makes them stand out from the rest. Beechnuts are a favorite food of wild turkeys which are again inhabiting the valley.

Another tree you see here is the white oak. Its bark is light grey and broken into irregular scales. A white oak can reach a height of 95 feet and is slow growing, living as long as 600 years! The oaks supply plenty of acorns for wildlife and depend on squirrels for propagation: the squirrels bury the acorns as a food cache, some of which sprout as young oaks.

Follow the path back to the field to complete your Forest Point walk.

KENDALL LAKE AREA

Kendall Lake is located in the Virginia Kendall Unit of Cuyahoga Valley National Recreation Area. The lake and surrounding hills act like a magnet to fishermen, hikers, and kite-flyers from spring through fall, and draw skiers, sledders, and snowmen makers in the winter. There is challenging hiking and skiing here and plenty of wide open spaces. Over 8 miles of trails lead into a variety of habitats: woodlands, hemlock ravines, fields, and wetlands. The Kendall Hills, above the lake, offer an excellent vantage point for enjoying autumn's color show.

The Kendall Lake area is part of what was formerly Virginia Kendall Metropolitan Park. In the early part of this century, Hayward Kendall, a wealthy Clevelander, owned these acres of forest and farmland and made them his country retreat. Kendall died in 1929, willing his land to be used for public park purposes. His will gave the first option to the National Park Service, which declined it, but the State of Ohio accepted the gift and the Akron Metropolitan Park District agreed to manage the park land. Later, in 1940, the State provided $75,000 for more acreage to be added to Kendall's 420 acres. The park was named Virginia Kendall, in memory of Kendall's mother.

The Civilian Conservation Corps (CCC) accomplished much of the early work of transforming the private retreat into a public park. Structures in the park built by the CCC in the 1930s include Kendall Lake itself, the Lake Shelter (originally used as a swimmers bathhouse and concession), restrooms, and toboggan chutes (later removed by the National Park Service due to safety concerns). In 1978, in an ironic turn of history, Virginia Kendall park was transferred to the National Park Service, which had declined it in 1929, so that it became the first federal unit of the new Cuyahoga Valley National Recreation Area.

This area is located about 2.5 miles south of Peninsula, on Truxell Road, midway between Akron Peninsula Road and Akron Cleveland Road.

36

2.5 miles

Skiing time: 1 hour

Hiking time: 1.5 hours

Elevation change:

160 feet

Moderate

Cross-country Trail

The Cross-country Trail was designed for skiing and makes equally good hiking. It winds through the area east of Kendall Lake, bounded by Truxell and Quick Roads. It is mostly in the woods but comes out onto Kendall Hills where there is lots of room to practice downhill runs (and falling). The ski trail is separated from the sledding hills, where you can find hundreds of sledders on a snowy weekend.

Most of this area was farmed at one time and even now you can see evidence of the fields, wood lots, farm lanes, and pastures. The mixture of woods and fields, hills and streams, supports much wildlife. Keep an eye out for mammals, from tiny meadow voles to white-tailed deer. Beaver have begun to use the lake, along with fish, frogs, mallards, and Canada geese. Many species of birds reside here due to the diversity of habitats.

You can best reach this trail from the Kendall Lake Shelter off Truxell Road but can also access it from Little Meadow Parking Area on Quick Road, just east of the sledding hills. The National Ski Patrol, operating out of a first aid hut at Kendall Hills, patrols the trail during ski season. There are plans to replace the first aid hut with a larger facility which will include all-season restrooms.

The Lake Shelter operates as the Winter Sports Center in January and February, offering information, hot drinks, and recreational programs. There are picnic tables and restrooms near the shelter. When hiking this trail during the skiing season, please observe the multi-use trail etiquette: refrain from hiking in the ski tracks, and yield to skiers, especially on hills. The Cross-country Trail is described in a clockwise direction from the start of the trail at the Lake Shelter parking lot.

Find the trail at the corner of the Lake Shelter parking lot, just to the left of the trailhead bulletin board. Enter the woods and climb up a fairly steep, open slope lined by pine trees. Partway up this slope, the Lake Trail crosses at right angles. After you gain the top of this slope, you

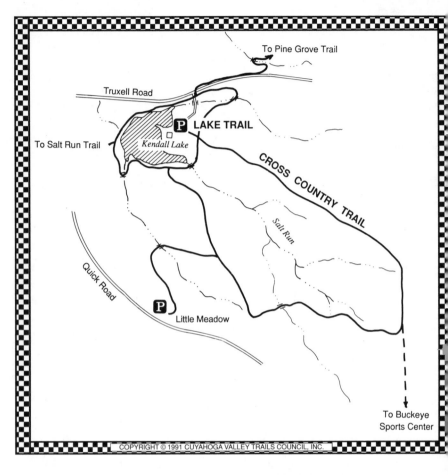

To Pine Grove Trail

Truxell Road

P LAKE TRAIL

To Salt Run Trail

Kendall Lake

CROSS COUNTRY TRAIL

Salt Run

Quick Road

P

Little Meadow

To Buckeye
Sports Center

Cross-Country Trail and Lake Trail

find the trail narrows to a two-person width and continues to climb more gradually. Pines and hardwoods make up the surrounding woods. Sweetgum trees, with their star-shaped leaves, are particularly attractive here in the autumn when the leaves turn yellow and orange on their way to a rich wine color. In pioneer days, the resin from these trees was used medicinally and for chewing gum. To the right of the trail is a stand of tulip trees recognized by their tall, straight trunks and tulip-shaped leaves.

At about three-quarters of a mile, you reach the location of a former farmstead. A large old white oak towers over the area, a remnant of earlier farming days. You can still find remains of old foundations in this area marked by clusters of daffodils in the spring. The surrounding area was a meadow, now well on its way to becoming forest again. The plentiful grasses, shrubs, and trees provide seeds and berries for juncos, field sparrows, grouse, rufous-sided towhees and other birds.

The trail curves and dips slightly to cross a tributary of Salt Run, the creek which feeds Kendall Lake. You then come to where the trail emerges from the woods and continues straight ahead bordered by a mature woods on the left and a meadow on the right. Follow this until the trail veers to the right to cross the meadow. The trail that continues straight leads to Buckeye Sports Center on Akron Cleveland Road. Bear to the right to stay on the Cross-country Trail. Your meadow crossing may be quick, as it can be hot in summer and bitter cold in winter! Its loveliest time is autumn, when goldenrods spread out in all directions.

At the far end of the meadow, reenter the woods and fairly soon begin the steep descent to Salt Run, crossing the creek on a bridge. This narrow descent can be tricky on skis and a strong "snowplow" and caution are urged so that you do not miss the bridge! The trail then uses an old roadbed to climb up out of the creek valley.

At the top of this hill, make a hairpin turn to the right (a service road straight ahead goes to Quick Road). Now once again high on a plateau, you pass through meadows that are becoming young forests through the process known as succession. Soon the trail splits at a "Y" intersection just after a bench. The branch to the left leads down a hill, across a stream, then across a field to Little Meadow Parking Area. The branch to the right is the continuation of the Cross-country Trail. Following it, you soon reach the top of the Kendall Hills, the lake shining in the distance below. Follow your instincts here—run, roll, plummet, plow, or plod down the hill in whatever way works best, aiming generally for the lake.

As you approach the lake, turn to the right to drop down and across Salt Run again. You can take the Lake Trail to the left to circle the lake, but this is suitable for skiing only partway. On the Cross-country Trail, you come to some graceful hemlock trees edging the lake just as you climb a hill to get around a small bay in the lake. At the top of the hill, go through a tunnel that was constructed to go under toboggan chutes. The 60 year old chutes were deteriorated and were removed in 1990.

After the tunnel, go straight ahead to rejoin the loop on the slope near where you started. A turn to the left takes you back to the parking lot.

37

Lake Trail

1 mile

Hiking time:

45 minutes

Elevation change:

minimal

Easy

The Lake Trail gives you close access to the entire circumference of Kendall Lake, beautiful in any season. The fairly level trail is suitable for a family stroll and offers good chances to see wildlife. Forest, stream, and lake meet here, providing a rich area for wild plant and animal life to flourish. The most common inhabitants found here are the Canada geese, and they share the lake and shores with many other bird species, insects, amphibians, and mammals. You might even see signs of beaver, as they have returned to the valley.

The Lake Shelter overlooks Kendall Lake. In January and February the shelter serves as a Winter Sports Center offering information, hot drinks, and a place to warm up. In other seasons, the shelter is available on a first-come, first-serve basis. The upper and lower porches are particularly nice for picnics, with the lake view framed by the shelter's stone walls. There are other picnic tables and benches on the lawn along the lake. Restrooms are located near the shelter. Fishing is permitted in the lake in the summertime, and the small pier is a good place for teaching children the fine art of placing the worm on the hook.

The Lake Trail leaves from the Kendall Lake Area parking lot off Truxell Road. Reach Truxell Road by going one mile south out of Peninsula on Akron Peninsula Road or one mile south of Route 303 on Akron Cleveland Road . The entrance to the Lake Area is about midway between Akron Peninsula and Akron Cleveland Roads.

Start the Lake Trail along with the Cross-country Trail; both leave from the southeast corner of the parking lot, near the trailhead bulletin board. Begin to climb the open slope, then turn to the right at the trail intersection to pass under the hill via a tunnel. The trail drops down along a bay of the lake then crosses Salt Run on a boardwalk. Shortly after this, the Cross-country Trail goes off to the left; to stay on the Lake Trail, continue ahead along the shores of the lake. With the lake to your right and the Kendall Hills to your left, the trail itself is shaded by a narrow band of trees. One of the most conspicuous trees is the American hornbeam, a good example of how confusing common names can be. Its sinewy, gray branches resemble muscles, suggesting one common name, muscle wood. It is a member of the birch family, but is also called water beech because it prefers moist soil and the bark resembles that of beech!

As you circle the lake, the view keeps changing. The small, quiet bays are favorite spots for birds and you may see the smaller of our common herons, the green-backed heron. About half-way around, cross the earthen dam which forms Kendall Lake from the waters of Salt Run. At the end of the dam, bear to the right and climb a set of steps to the hill above the shoreline. Mature beech trees here frame the Lake Shelter in the distance. Rattlesnake weed, identified by its striking purple veined leaves, can be found clinging to these slopes, along with club mosses. The club mosses are notable as they are one of the most ancient plants on earth, dating back at least 400 million years!

Descend a short way, climb again, then descend steps to reach the backwaters of the lake. Here is one of the places along the shore where you might be able to spot signs of beaver activity such as sharply pointed, gnawed stumps of saplings. Continue across the Kendall Lake entrance drive and through a swamp. Here in the cattails and tree stumps, red-winged blackbirds and woodpeckers claim their territories. Sounds announce the seasons, with spring peepers proclaiming the return of spring and the dry rustle of cattails ushering in winter.

Leave the swamp by crossing the creek, then climb steps into a planted pine forest. Rejoin the Cross-country Trail on the open slope where you began. Turn to the right to reach the parking lot.

38

🚶

4.4 miles

Hiking time: 2 hours

Elevation change:

160 feet

Moderate to difficult

Salt Run Trail

Salt Run Trail, west of Kendall Lake, takes a long route through the forested, rugged hills drained by Salt Run. The length and terrain make this trail more challenging than others in the area, and it can be combined with the Lake and Cross-country Trails for an even longer hike. The short-cut loop on the Salt Run Trail offers a less challenging alternative hike. Both the long and short routes take you through pine, oak, hickory, beech, and hemlock areas. A variety of ferns, including the evergreen Christmas fern, and many wildflowers border the trail.

Begin the Salt Run Trail from Pine Hollow parking area at Kendall Hills on Quick Road. Quick Road is 1.4 miles south of Peninsula and runs between Akron Peninsula and Akron Cleveland Roads. You can also reach Salt Run Trail from the Kendall Lake parking lot on Truxell Road. There are picnic tables, grills, and outhouses at the start of the trail at Pine Hollow.

From the Pine Hollow parking area, walk past the trail sign at the northwest end of the lot, across the top of the hill, and into the pine woods. To reach the trail from Kendall Lake, follow the Lake Trail to the far side of the lake then go out onto the Kendall Hills and climb the hill at the edge of the forest to reach the trailhead. Enter the woods at the trail sign.

Following the trail clockwise, bear to the left onto the footpath and descend to cross a stream on a small bridge. Climbing out of this creek valley, continue through a mixed forest for less than .25 mile, then out onto Quick Road in order to get around the head of a narrow ravine. Walk along the road for 70 yards, then follow the trail back into the woods.

About 1 mile from the start, you reach the short-cut trail. Follow this to your right for a shorter loop. This area where the short-cut intersects was still a clearing in the

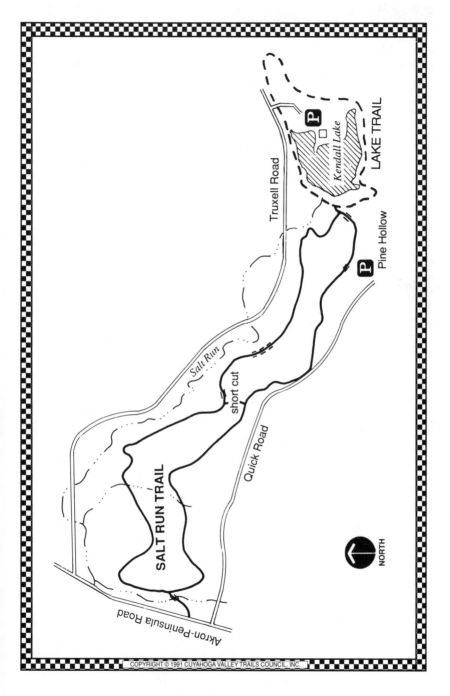

Salt Run Trail

1960s. You can still detect the difference between this former clearing and the surrounding forest.

Shortly past the cut-off, you reach a wooden bench overlooking the deciduous forest, then begin a steep drop to the lowlands. A large, old oak tree here in the valley appears to have escaped the saw, and the aging fruit trees nearby now provide food for wildlife. Next is a steady, short climb to White Oak Spring, a natural spring occurring at the base of a white oak tree. Continuing on, you reach another bench, then again descend a steep slope to the valley floor. Now near Akron Peninsula Road, the trail follows the route of the older East River Road for a short way. A tributary of Salt Run is on the left, and a side trail (part of a Boy Scout loop trail) joins in from Akron Peninsula Road.

Just before reaching Salt Run, the trail turns to the right and goes into a thicket of young deciduous trees. These are slowly replacing the scrubby meadow that was here in the 1960s. Being in the lowlands of Salt Run, the trail can be very muddy, but the surrounding wet habitat supports some interesting plants. Mosses, often producing the first green of spring, adorn the rocks and tree trunks. Jewelweed thrives here in the summer along with wild grapes, thistles, goldenrods, and thorn apples. Because of the food and cover, this is a good area for seeing birds and deer. Past this section and on up a narrow ridge, you come to where the short-cut rejoins the main trail.

Past the short-cut, drop down a steep slope then cross a long bridge. You are still in the floodplain of Salt Run. In this creek valley, you come to an area of hemlocks and beeches on an "island" of land separated by drainage cuts in the landscape. Here you can often see remnants of mud slides, exposing clay soils. Many of the slopes in the valley are unstable, and you can find evidence of their movements where slumps like these occur. Cross side creeks via three bridges, then follow along the hemlock island into a lovely hemlock ravine. Here the evergreen hemlocks reach heights of 30-50 feet.

Climb out of the hemlock ravine and along a planted pine forest. From the top of this hill, you can see Kendall Lake when the leaves are off the trees. Bear to the right to follow the trail (it has been rerouted in recent years—the old trail went straight ahead). You can find some good sized oaks here, as they do best on these high, dry ridges. Again, bear to the right, coming down to the foot of the sledding hills. Kendall Lake is to your left. Turn right, reenter the pine woods, and climb the hill to reach the end of the trail at Pine Hollow parking lot.

DEEP LOCK QUARRY METRO PARK

Deep Lock Quarry Metro Park is owned and maintained by Metro Parks, Serving Summit County, which acquired the 77-acre park in 1934. Deep Lock contains remains of the valley's quarry, canal, and railroad operations from the early 1800s to the early 1900s. The main natural feature is a lovely fast-water stretch of the Cuyahoga River; two main historic features are the Berea Sandstone Quarry and Deep Lock (Lock 28 on the Ohio and Erie Canal). In 1879 Ferdinand Schumacher owned a part of the quarry, finding that the sandstone made good millstones for his American Cereal Works in Akron (later Quaker Oats). Discarded millstones are found throughout the park. Stones cut from this quarry also provided building blocks for the canal locks and many local structures. Deep Lock on the Ohio and Erie Canal is the deepest lock between Akron and Cleveland and is in good condition.

During the heyday of the canal and quarrying era, pioneers stripped this area of its trees. It is now mostly reforested and has one of the finest concentrations of Ohio buckeye trees in the county. The buckeye, Ohio's state tree, is most conspicuous in the spring when it displays 6-inch long, upright flower clusters. In the fall, children (and many adults) enjoy picking up the smooth, brown seed that resembles a buck's eye.

The old canal bed still holds some shallow water. On warm spring days, turtles sun themselves while the croaking of bullfrogs echoes off the lock walls. A shallow swamp at the base of the quarry features many plants including the infrequently found narrow-leaved cattail and rose pink. This area is also a popular spot for birders. During the spring migrations, you may spot warblers, flycatchers, orioles, vireos, sparrows, finches, and perhaps a thrush or a brilliant scarlet tanager. Along the river you might see great blue herons, geese, kingfishers, and woodpeckers. This is a small area, but with much to see!

Deep Lock Quarry has two hiking trails, the Quarry Trail and the Towpath Trail. Both loop trails overlap each other and could be walked as one trail. A portion of the Buckeye Trail also passes through the park; it is marked with a blue BT in a directional arrow. Picnic sites and toilets are located just off the parking lot.

Reach Deep Lock Quarry Metro Park by going south out of Peninsula on Riverview Road. The entrance drive is .75 miles south of Route 303.

39

🚶

1.3 miles

Hiking time:

45 minutes

Elevation change:

120 feet

Easy to moderate

Towpath Trail in Deep Lock

The Towpath Trail in Deep Lock is a short loop trail that incorporates part of the canal towpath, as distinguished from the much longer, 20+ mile Towpath Trail which is the major north-south spine trail in CVNRA. "Towpath" signifies the path that lines the canal and was used by the mules as they towed the canal boats.

In Deep Lock Quarry, start the Towpath Trail from the north edge of the parking lot. It is marked by the Metro Park "step" symbol. From the parking lot, follow the wide trail down towards the railroad tracks used by the Cuyahoga Valley Line excursion train. Go on past the sign post; the trail levels off and is bordered by scattered millstones and small mounds which are from the quarrying days when workers scraped soil off the underlying sandstone to expose it for cutting.

At the next sign post the two trails split; follow Towpath Trail to the right, descending to the canal bed and Deep Lock. Lock 28 is 17 feet deep (locks were usually no more than 12 to 14 feet deep); all the workings of the lock are gone now, however, iron guides for the balance beams that opened and closed the main gate remain at each end of the lock.

The southern end of the lock is dry; cross here to the other side. At this point the Buckeye Trail joins the Towpath Trail. Partially visible off to the right are the remains of other sandstone canal structures. Follow the Towpath Trail back along the edge of the lock then descend to parallel the Cuyahoga River.

At the next trail junction, the Buckeye Trail goes straight north towards Peninsula, staying on the longer Towpath Trail, while this Towpath loop trail turns off to the left and crosses the canal. From here, climb up the hill and join the Quarry Trail. Follow both trails to the left, along a ridge above the river.

Along this path you can still find pieces of the old railroad siding leading into the quarry. The trail now follows that old railroad bed, turning away from the river and into the base of the quarry itself.

After exploring the quarry, leave the area via the Towpath Trail on a wide path heading south. (The Quarry Trail goes in the opposite direction, looping up around the top of the quarry). At the next junction, turn to the right and go up a small hill past other old quarry-related foundations. Rejoin the original trail just at the foot of the first hill. Turn right to climb the hill to the parking lot.

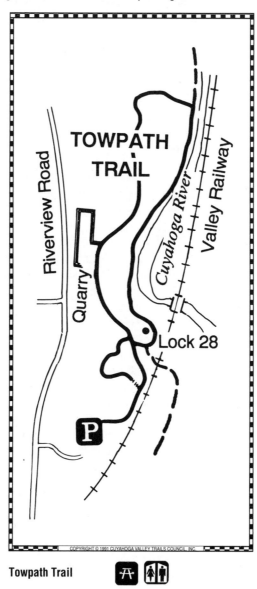

Towpath Trail

40

Quarry Trail

1.2 miles

Hiking time:

35-45 minutes

Elevation change:

120 feet

Easy to moderate

The Quarry Trail makes a loop through the remains of the Berea Sandstone quarry that furnished much of the stone for local foundations and canal locks. Begin this trail along with the Towpath Trail, from the Deep Lock Metro Park parking lot. Descend the hill and follow the trail straight ahead. At the trail junction, continue straight on the Quarry Trail towards the quarry; the Towpath Trail, branching to the right, leads to Deep Lock. Once at the quarry, step with caution as the stones are often wet and slippery.

The quarry, opened in 1829, provided sandstone for many regional structures including the first section of Akron City Hospital. It was also used in building the breakwall in Cleveland, along with the intake crib in Lake Erie where Cleveland's water supply inlet is located. After 1879, Ferdinand Schumacher began using the stones as hulling stones at his American Cereal Works in Akron (later to become Quaker Oats). Schumacher is credited with introducing oatmeal to America, so these stones deserve a place of honor in America's breakfast history!

Early quarrying was slow, difficult work performed with hand tools. Workers risked their share of occupational hazards, including lung diseases from inhaling the fine grit. Small sponges tied under the noses of quarry workers were the precursors of today's masks. Late in the 1880s, the introduction of mechanization altered the quarrying process. One of the new machines was a channeling machine driven by a steam engine. It traveled on a portable track, driving bits against the stone, which cut a channel about three inches wide. By cutting such channels at right angles, the stone could be "cubed", the bottom side loosened by wedges or a small blast. You can see evidence of the use of this machine in the smooth sides of the rock face and exposed channel marks in the quarry sandstone.

After exploring the quarry bottom, leave via the Quarry Trail by turning to the right of the exposed walls. Follow the sign to the quarry rim, climbing the hill on some steep steps. From the rim, you gain a full view of the quarry area. Again, be careful when climbing around the steep- walled quarry. Now follow the Quarry Trail away from the rim; it bears to the right and soon joins the Towpath Trail. Both trails turn south to reenter the quarry along the route of an old railroad spur. Exit the quarry the way you came in, going south on the wide trail. At the next junction, turn to the right and go up a small hill past other old quarry-related foundations. Rejoin the original trail just at the foot of the first hill. Turn right to climb the hill to the parking lot.

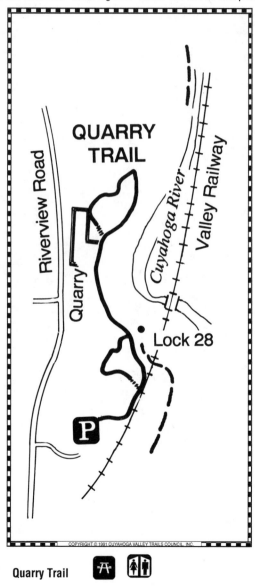

QUARRY TRAIL

Riverview Road

Quarry

Cuyahoga River

Valley Railway

Lock 28

P

Quarry Trail

Tree Farm Trail

OAK HILL

This upland plateau contains one of the largest roadless areas of contiguous federally owned land in the recreation area. The area is dotted by numerous small ponds and contains stands of native (mature) oak and hickory, meadows, pine plantations, and a former Christmas tree farm. Two trailheads serve the area, each with a small loop trail.

At the southern end of the Oak Hill area, the National Park Service is developing the Cuyahoga Valley Environmental Education Center. The entire center is considered an outdoor classroom, therefore, should you happen upon a class in session, please be considerate and do not interrupt. Fishing in the three small ponds behind the center is "reserved for wildlife". Fishermen can try their luck at one of four other public ponds in the Oak Hill area — Meadowedge, Sylvan, Goosefeather or Horseshoe.

41

2.75 miles

Skiing time:

45 minutes

Hiking time: 1.5 hours

Elevation change:

80 feet

Easy to moderate

Tree Farm Trail

Tree Farm Trail traverses what was part of the Robert Bishop family Christmas tree farm. This was a "cut your own" tree farm. In December, cars would line Major Road as people would hunt for their special Christmas tree. The Bishops have roots far back into Peninsula history, and Robert Bishop's daughter continues family tradition by operating a tree farm on part of the original acreage. Although the trail is entirely on public land, it approaches near to the Bishop's private property. Please respect these property lines when exploring this lovely trail.

The topography here is gently rolling and the ski trail is wide with generally good sight lines, making this an excellent novice to intermediate level trail. Some second growth hardwoods and large open fields with good views of the valley interrupt the broad stands of evergreens. Snow laden evergreen tunnels add to the appeal of this trail. Though bordered by two roads and the village of Peninsula, you will usually find the trail conveys a feeling of quiet and remoteness.

Wildlife is abundant here due to diversity of shelter and food. It is possible to see deer, fox, and coyote. This is also excellent bird habitat, and a keen eye may spot several species of warblers, yellow-breasted chats, cedar waxwings, cardinals, bobolinks, hawks, and owls.

Tree Farm Trail is located on Major Road off Riverview Road, .5 mile south of Peninsula. From Riverview Road, it is .8 mile to the trailhead, marked as Horseshoe Pond. Horseshoe Pond is a popular fishing pond, where lucky anglers catch bass or bluegill. There is a small parking lot here but no developed facilities. The trail begins from the parking area and is a loop trail. It is described here in a clockwise direction to get the best views.

From the parking area, follow the trail to the earthen dam of Horseshoe Pond, then across the dam itself. At the end of the dam, watch for the trail sign indicating a turn into the woods to the right. This begins a gently rolling and curving section of trail that uses some of the old tree farm lanes.

After about a half-mile, you come into a more open area where brambles and multiflora rose repel hikers and entice birds. Soon after, the trail breaks out into an open field. Follow the path to the top of the open knoll at an elevation of 890 feet; here you can see across the valley to the east. The high points on the opposite rim are at the Ledges Area. Closer by and just below, you can see the neatly planted rows of evergreens at the tree farm.

Descend the hill and cross a former farm lane lined with trees. Continue on through second growth woods, then drop down a small hill to cross a stream via a bridge. A bench further along the way is a good spot to sit and watch for deer.

You are about half-way around the trail and fairly close to Riverview Road at this point. The latter half of the trail continues a winding course through evergreens and along sumac and dogwood shrub thickets. You are paralleling Riverview Road, then Major Road. Follow the trail as it curves away from Major Road, then in and out of evergreens again, using the farm lanes.

Near the end of the trail you come out of one of these lanes towards an open field; turn sharply to the right. Descend this slope and turn left to go back into the evergreens. Come out into the open again, bear to the right and cross a small freshet on a bridge. The pond is to the right, and in a few yards you reach the parking lot where you began.

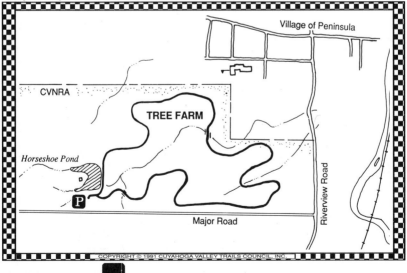

Tree Farm Trail

42

1.5 miles

Hiking time:

45 minutes

Skiing time:

30 minutes

Elevation change:

50 feet

Easy

Oak Hill Trail

The National Park Service opened the Oak Hill Day Use Area in 1983. It has been partially developed, offering a small picnic area, fishing, and hiking. A picnic shelter and another trail are in the plans for this area. Oak Hill Trail is known for its two ponds, Meadowedge and Sylvan, plus its meadows and second growth upland woods of mostly oaks and hickories. The trail is designed for easy hiking or cross-country skiing. It can be quite muddy in places after rains—hiking boots are recommended. There are several stream crossings, all on bridges or boardwalk.

A Youth Conservation Corps crew cleared this trail originally, then when the Cuyahoga Valley Trails Council was established, the council adopted this trail and has made several improvements including bridges and a boardwalk. The National Park Service has rebuilt the dams on both ponds plus a third pond, Goosefeather, located just north of Oak Hill on Scobie Road. All these ponds are good for fishing and ideal for introducing young people to the beauty and delight of pond life.

The Oak Hill Day Use Area is south of Peninsula. From Riverview Road turn west onto Major Road. From Major Road, turn onto Oak Hill Road. The entrance drive to the area is one mile down Oak Hill Road.

The loop trail starts from the eastern edge of the parking lot at the trailhead bulletin board. Less than a half-mile walk in either direction will bring you to one of the ponds.

Taking the trail to the right (toward Meadowedge Pond), in a counterclockwise direction, start out along a former farm field. Since the field is no longer used for agriculture, it is being revegetated naturally in a process called succession. Right now it is mostly grasses and wildflowers, habitat for butterflies, birds, small mammals, and many other creatures. If natural changes are allowed to continue, the grasses will be replaced by shrubs, then forest.

Some of the plants you may find in this and other meadows are orange hawkweed and oxeye daisy in the spring, followed by the colorful mix of Queen Anne's lace, goldenrod, and ironweed in the late summer and fall.

Continuing on the trail you reach a young forest of oaks and hawthorns, cross a small stream via a bridge, then come into another meadow. This meadow is periodically mowed in order to maintain the diversity of habitats, allowing the area to have a number of fields in varying stages of succession.

Beyond the meadow, bear to the left to reach Meadowedge Pond. This little pond is typical of man-made farm ponds. It is a lovely spot any time of year. In the warm months, you can listen to harrumphs of bullfrogs and the chickaree of red-winged blackbirds while watching dragonflies catch a meal over the water.

Follow the sign back into the woods to continue the loop (not around the pond). This area was planted with trees some years ago, evidenced by the straight rows of trunks. Further along is an area where the trail has been "turnpiked" to try to keep it drier underfoot. Descend to cross the creek again, then follow the trail into an older oak/hickory/maple woods. From here the trail goes through a pine woods, then bears to the left to come out of the woods along Sylvan Pond.

The trail crosses the dam of this larger, attractive pond, then reenters the woods. Continue another 10 to 15 minutes through the woods, into a shrubby area, and onto the boardwalk over a swampy area. The trail ends just beyond, at the parking lot.

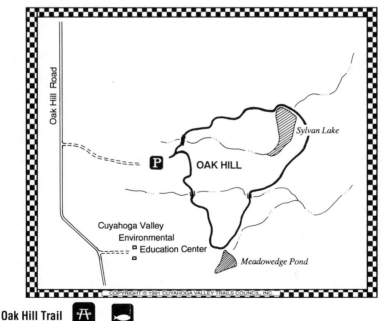

Oak Hill Trail

Langes Run Trail

WETMORE BRIDLE TRAIL SYSTEM

The Wetmore Trailhead is the starting place for five interconnected trails designed primarily for horseback riding. The trails, located on both sides of Wetmore Road, cross the wooded ridges and stream bottoms of Dickerson Run and Langes Run, an area once used for raising horses. Scattered throughout the area are old barns, pastures, shelters and horse pastures, reminders of the earlier farming days. Selecting different combinations of these trails allows you to plan rides or hikes from 1 mile to 11 miles or more.

The name Wetmore dates back to Frederick and Emila Wetmore, landowners here in the late 1800s. Several owners have succeeded them, the most recent being a nationally recognized breeder of Morgan and thoroughbred horses. Some of this land was acquired by Metro Parks, Serving Summit County, then in 1984 the National Park Service purchased the remainder of the farms. The current trails follow old logging roads and horse paths used by previous owners. Much of the trail routing and clearing was accomplished by volunteers from the Ohio Horsemen's Council and the Cuyahoga Valley Trails Council in cooperation with the National Park Service. The Horsemen's Council continues to do maintenance on the trails in partnership with the National Park Service trail crew.

At the time of this writing, plans were underway to build a similar bridle trail system on the opposite side of the Cuyahoga Valley in the Riding Run area. A trail across the Cuyahoga River will connect the two trail systems, allowing for long, all-day trail rides.

To reach the Wetmore Trailhead, travel south out of Peninsula on Akron Peninsula Road. Wetmore Road is the third road to the left, 1.75 miles from Peninsula. The parking lot is located one-half mile up the road. The parking lot has ample space for horse trailers. At the time of this publication, there were no picnic facilities at the trailhead.

43

4 miles

Riding time: 1.5 hours

Elevation change:

250 feet

Moderate

Wetmore Trail

Wetmore Trail starts at the trailhead bulletin board at the east end of the Wetmore Trailhead parking lot. Situated entirely between Wetmore and Quick Roads, the trail's 4 miles goes through most of the area drained by Dickerson Run. The bottom lands here can be very muddy, especially in the spring.

From the trailhead bulletin board, follow the trail down along the fenced pastures and into a mixed woods of aspens, red maples and sycamores. In about .25 mile you will come to the sign indicating the start of the Wetmore Trail loop—take the circular trail in either direction at this point. Our description will follow the trail to the right (counterclockwise).

Here in the lowlands the trail crosses bridges over tributaries of Dickerson Run and passes fields that were formerly pastures. It can be <u>very</u> muddy in this section. Follow the fence line until you reach the intersection with the Dickerson Run Trail. Here the Wetmore Trail turns uphill, away from the creek, and enters a forested area. At the top of this ridge you find fairly level ground for about 1 mile. Even this high ground can be quite muddy where it is not well drained. Dickerson Run valley is off to your right but well out of sight.

Along this high ground, you come to the intersection with Dickerson Run Trail coming in on your right, then Tabletop Trail going off to the left. Continue on Wetmore Trail in a generally south to southeast direction. About halfway around the 4-mile loop, you enter an area of planted trees, mostly white and red pines and spruces, pass over a bridge spanning a tributary, then follow along a large meadow until you reach the other end of Tabletop Trail. Go past this intersection and past a tiny pond which is slowly silting in.

Leaving the meadow and high ground, descend into the bottom lands and cross a bridge. Come out of the creek valley on an uphill stretch of trail, then parallel Quick Road, now heading northwest. Grasses, field wildflowers and young tulip trees favor these sunnier, open sections of the trail.

After paralleling Quick Road for about one-half mile, the trail turns left to drop down to the bottom lands. Follow this down and across a branch of Dickerson Run. Cross a second time, then leave the valley on a relatively steep climb. Large old oak trees dominate the ridge here, and if the branches are bare you can glimpse the meandering course of the stream below.

Soon you reach a switchback down into the stream valley. At the bottom, cross the stream and bear to the right, past a thicket of Ohio buckeye trees. This state tree of Ohio can be recognized by its five leaflets forming a single leaf. In early spring, the buckeye's large buds swell and open to reveal inner greenish and rose scales. The five part leaflet emerges fanlike, followed by pale yellow-green flower clusters. Even more familiar to Ohioans, however, is the tree's fruit—a thick, prickly round capsule which breaks open to release the shiny, brown nut resembling a "buck's eye."

Follow the trail on a short climb out of the bottom land and into an old pasture. You might see deer here—watch for the white flag of their tail as they signal alarm. At the signpost, you have completed the 4-mile loop; turn right to climb back up to the parking lot.

44

1 mile

Riding time:

20 minutes

Elevation change:

175 feet

Easy to moderate

Dickerson Run Trail

Dickerson Run Trail, in the Wetmore Bridle Trail System, is only 1 mile, but you must take Wetmore Trail to reach it, so the overall length is at least 2.5 miles. The trail follows Dickerson Run; half of the distance is in the creek valley, the other half on the ridge above the stream.

To reach Dickerson Run Trail, start from the Wetmore Trailhead bulletin board. Follow the trail down to where the Wetmore Trail splits to the right and left (less than .25 mile). Turn to the right and go about another .25 mile to the intersection of Dickerson Run and Wetmore Trails.

Turn to the right to begin Dickerson Run Trail. For the first .5 mile or so, the trail stays in the stream lowlands and can be quite muddy. There are rewards, however. Many wildflowers thrive in these wet places, and you can also find several different fern species, including the delicate black stemmed maidenhair fern.

About halfway on Dickerson Run Trail you begin the climb out of the creek valley and onto the ridge. In fall and winter there are some nice views off to the right. Langes Run Trail comes in from the right near the intersection with Wetmore Trail. Climb some more, through planted pines, just before joining the Wetmore Trail. At this point you have several options for returning to the trailhead. Turning to the left on Wetmore Trail is the shortest way back. Longer trips can be made taking Wetmore in the other direction or Langes Run Trail to the southwest.

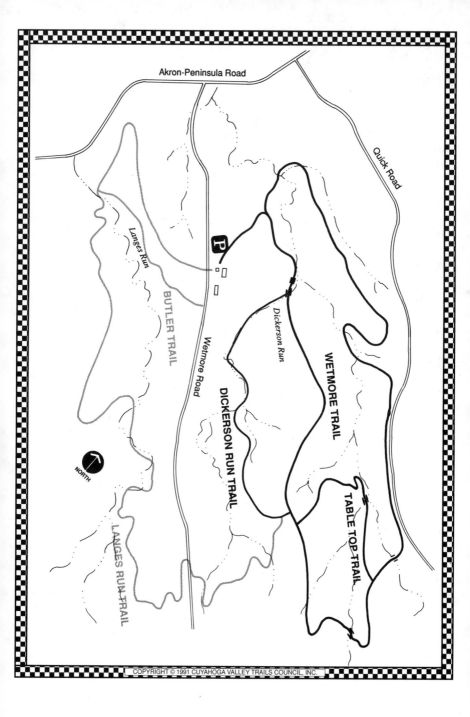

Wetmore Trail, Dickerson Run Trail, and Tabletop Trail

45

.75 mile

Riding time:

20 minutes

Elevation change:

100 feet

Easy to moderate

Tabletop Trail

Tabletop Trail, in the Wetmore Bridle Trail System, is only .75 mile long, but to reach it you must travel 1.5 miles; round trips are about 4.5 miles. This trail follows the high "tabletop" plateau of land between the branches of Dickerson Run and includes a steep descent and climb at its western end.

To reach the start of Tabletop Trail, follow Wetmore Trail from the trailhead bulletin board .25 mile, then turn to the right where Wetmore Trail splits to begin its loop. Go 1.5 miles on Wetmore Trail to reach the start of Tabletop Trail which goes off to the left just past the junction with Dickerson Run Trail.

Tabletop Trail goes through a corridor of white pines, red maples, and flowering dogwoods before entering an oak-hickory forest. The beautiful white blossoms of the dogwood line this trail in the spring, and in the fall witch hazel closes out the season with its tiny yellow blossoms. All along this trail is an abundant supply of nuts and acorns supplying food for many squirrels and chipmunks. Follow this level tabletop to a switchback down to the stream.

Cross the stream on a wooden bridge, then climb out of the valley through a beech-maple woods. The trail finishes on high ground, rejoining the Wetmore Trail at the edge of a pasture. To return to the trailhead, take Wetmore Trail in either direction, about 2 miles either way.

46

4 .5 miles

Riding time:

1.5 to 2 hours

Elevation change:

190 feet

Moderate to difficult

Langes Run Trail

Langes Run Trail in the Wetmore Bridle Trail System includes a bit of everything: high meadows, ponds, stream bottom lands, and steep, wooded slopes. To make a loop trip, combine this trail with Dickerson Run and Wetmore Trails (6-9 miles depending on your chosen route).

To begin Langes Run Trail, leave the Wetmore Trailhead parking area and cross Wetmore Road. A sign indicates the start of the trail, on an old farm lane. Follow the mowed path through the pasture. At about 870-foot elevation, there are good views of the valley to the west. Nestled in the fields are two farm ponds. The fields themselves are full of sun-loving plants.

At the far end of the meadow, the trail begins to descend into the woods. At the bottom of the slope follow an old fence line bordering a cultivated field. Akron Peninsula Road can be seen beyond the field. While still down in the lowlands, you come to the intersection with Butler Trail. Continuing on Langes Run Trail, cross Langes Run then climb a hill to an oak-hickory forest.

The trail stays in the woods until coming to a utility right-of-way clearing. Turn left into the clearing, then in a short distance, turn right, back into the woods. A long stretch of mud can be found here even in dry weather. Next, the trail goes through a meadow in succession. Aspens are pioneer species here, helping revert the meadow to forest. Still on the ridge, you come into a dense woods of maples, ashes, tulip trees, and sassafras.

Descend once again to the stream valley; you are at the midway point on the trail. The meandering nature of Langes Run is soon evident as you cross it several times. There is a large sycamore tree just before the trail begins to switchback up the hillside. At the top, enter the oak-hickory forest, crossing the high ground between the drainages, then follow the trail back down to the floodplain. In a short distance, climb again, coming out to Wetmore Road.

Cross Wetmore Road and continue on Langes Run Trail. After crossing a field, the trail turns right, bordering the edge of a ravine, then comes out onto a private driveway. Turn left and follow the driveway for a short distance, then left again into the woods. After the woods you go into a large meadow, then descend to cross Dickerson Run. Finally, climb out of this valley and reach the end of Langes Run Trail where it intersects with Dickerson Run Trail.

To return to the parking lot, follow the Dickerson Run or Wetmore Trail.

47

Butler Trail

.75 mile

Riding time:

20 minutes

Elevation change:

150 feet

Easy

Butler Trail, part of the Wetmore Bridle Trail System, connects Langes Run Trail to Wetmore Road, partially using an old brick road. Reach the trail by following Langes Run Trail for 1 mile to where the two trails intersect or by following Wetmore Road southeast (left out of the parking lot) for about 800 feet.

Accessing the trail from Langes Run Trail, turn left onto Butler Trail. For about half its length, Butler Trail follows the meanders of Langes Run through a wet bottom land habitat of cottonwood and sycamore trees. Coltsfoot, an early spring wildflower, is abundant in this area.

Cross Langes Run twice, then climb out of the valley on a brick road which was once a connection between Wetmore and Akron Peninsula Roads. The trail ends at Wetmore Road. Turn left to return to the Wetmore Trailhead.

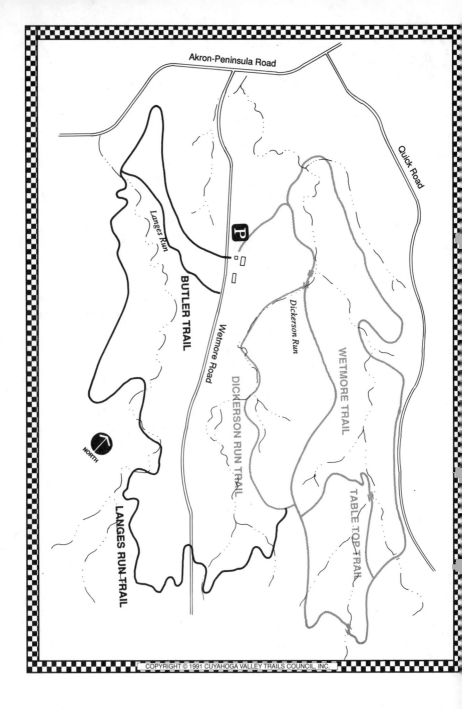

Langes Run Trail and Butler Trail

HAMPTON HILLS METRO PARK

Hampton Hills Metro Park is within the boundaries of the Cuyahoga Valley National Recreation Area but is owned and managed by Metro Parks, Serving Summit County. The rugged topography from the floor of the Cuyahoga Valley to the eastern ridge makes the hiking here moderate to difficult. You can also find a variety of habitats here including streams, ravines, fields and forests. This "park with all the bridges" is very popular with children because of the many log bridges spanning Adam Run and its side creeks. Many of these bridges were washed out by high water in 1989 but have been replaced.

The 278 acres of Hampton Hills were acquired in two main parcels. In 1964 the City of Akron leased 116 acres of wooded ravines along Akron Peninsula Road to the park district in exchange for land at Goodyear Heights Metropolitan Park where the city wished to erect a water tower. In 1967, Rhea H. and E. Reginald Adam donated to the park district 162 acres of ravines and their hilltop farm, including their century old farmhouse. The farm area is known as Top O' The World—for good reason, as you will see when you visit the area. There are two trails in Hampton Hills, Adam Run Trail and Spring Hollow Trail; Adam Run Trail is the newest, constructed by the Youth Conservation Corps in 1979. Both trails leave from the edge of the main parking lot.

Hampton Hills is located in Cuyahoga Falls on Akron Peninsula Road between Steels Corners Road and Bath Road. The main entrance and parking area are located on Akron Peninsula Road just north of the intersection with Bath Road. Another entrance, primarily used by visitors to the Top O' The World area, is located on Bath Road east of Akron Peninsula Road. A picnic area (with grills but no water) and toilets are located near the main parking lot. A soccer field and ballfield, off Steels Corners Road, can be used by obtaining a permit from Metro Parks, Serving Summit County.

48

3.2 miles

Hiking time:

1 1/2 to 2 hours

Elevation change:

230 feet

Moderate to difficult

due to steep climbs

Adam Run Trail

Adam Run and Spring Hollow Trails both start out together. They are described in a clockwise direction. Adam Run Trail is marked by the Metro Parks stream symbol on sign posts along the way.

Find the entrance to both trails at the edge of the parking lot away from Akron Peninsula Road. Bear to the left to begin the loop. When you start out on these trails, you are following the old East River Road which was relocated and renamed Akron Peninsula Road in the late 1920s, and you cross an interesting iron-railed bridge that was part of East River Road. Other remnants of this old road can be found up and down the valley between Bath Road and Peninsula.

During the first half mile or so, follow the Adam Run valley upstream, crossing the creek eight times on bridges. The creek valley is a good area for spring wildflowers and for an unusual looking plant with hollow, evergreen, grooved stems. These are scouring rushes, in the genus of plants called Equisetum. Equisetums are in a category of plants that thrived and dominated plant life 180-500 million years ago. Only this genus survives today. The common name for this plant comes from the fact that they have been used for scouring or polishing, having silica in the stems. The rushes are often found along stream borders where their underground horizontal branching system can help anchor the soil along the banks.

After about a half mile, the two trails split. Bear left to stay on Adam Run Trail which follows the main course of the stream. Continue to climb the ravine; as it steepens, 91 steps built into the steep hillside makes your climb a little easier! A Civilian Conservation Corps style bench at the top is a good place to enjoy the views into the ravines full of black walnuts, elms and sycamores. As you continue, the trail climbs at a gentler grade before passing through a white pine plantation planted by Girl Scouts in 1968.

After the pines, you come out into the open and crisscross fields and old fence rows. These fields and fence rows create an edge effect which is favored by birds and other wildlife. In the fall, goldenrods gild these fields with their arching, golden branches. By now you have climbed near the top of the east ridge of the valley and can begin to enjoy the views off to the west. Two benches are located on the trail; the second is near where a side trail enters from Top O' The World area. This side trail takes you to the former farm house which is maintained as an example of mid-1800s Western Reserve style of architecture. You can still see the farm pond, orchard, and fields which now feed a variety of wild, rather than domesticated, inhabitants.

After leaving this area, follow the trail through a young woods and across three more bridges. Right after the third bridge, Adam Run Trail rejoins Spring Hollow Trail. Together these trails wind their way back down to the valley below, first going through an area which is changing from field to forest through the process of succession. As you head back into the valley, sets of steps make the descent a little easier. You end this hike along a section of trail that again follows the old East River Road alignment, leading back to the parking lot.

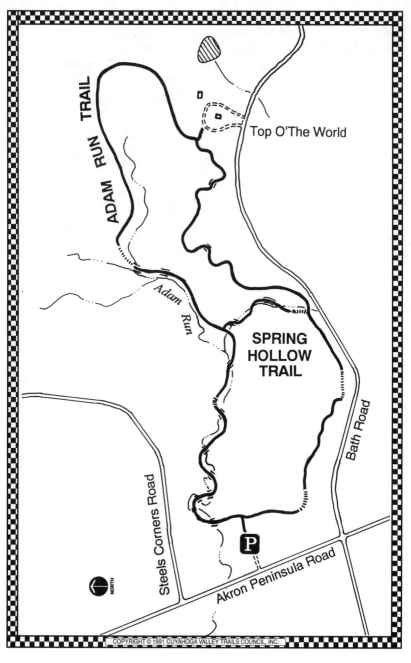

Top O'The World

ADAM RUN TRAIL

Adam Run

SPRING HOLLOW TRAIL

Bath Road

Steels Corners Road

Akron Peninsula Road

P

NORTH

Adam Run Trail and Spring Hollow Trail

49

1.6 miles

Hiking time: 1 hour

Elevation change:

150 feet

Moderate

Spring Hollow Trail

Spring Hollow Trail starts out along with Adam Run Trail, both following the route of the former East River Road. This road was relocated and is now Akron Peninsula Road. Following Spring Hollow Trail, clockwise, wind your way up the Adam Run valley, crossing and recrossing the creek 8 times. In just over a half-mile, the two trails split; for Spring Hollow go straight ahead, continuing along a creek. It is marked by Metro Park signs with a symbol of an oak leaf.

You now head up a deep, picturesque ravine. There are many fallen trees along the steep banks, with several straddling the narrow stream bed. A 50 foot boardwalk makes the going easier over the stream soaked base of the ravine. There are also a couple more log bridges crossing this side creek. The last gasp climb to the top of the ravine has a total of 76 steps and rises more than 50 feet.

At the top of the hill, rejoin Adam Run Trail which enters from the left. The two trails, now joined, cross a scrub meadow area. The meadow still has berry bushes, but is slowly but surely becoming forest once again. Just after entering the woods again, begin the descent back down into the valley; two sets of steps makes the going a little easier. You can find plenty of large oaks up on the drier upland sections of this trail, and walnuts, slippery elms, maples and sycamores in the wetter ravines. In places, wild grape vines have created openings in the forest canopy where you might find birds feasting on the grapes. The last stretch of this trail is on the old East River Road alignment; it then ends at the parking lot where you began.

O'NEIL WOODS METRO PARK

O'Neil Woods was acquired by Metro Parks, Serving Summit County, in 1969 when the family of the late William and Grace O'Neil leased their family farm to the park district, then later donated the farm outright, for public use and enjoyment. The O'Neil family had enjoyed the farm for two decades, using it for gentleman farming, horseback riding, and family outings.

A picnic grove is now located near the remains of the barn. Part of the foundation and an animal trough are still there, though overgrown. Picnic tables, grills, and pit toilets are all near the parking lot. A large old white pine stands sentinel over the "Lone Pine" area where you start and end Deer Run Trail, the only trail in O'Neil Woods Metro Park.

50

🚶

1.8 mile

Hiking time: 1 hour

Elevation change:

200 feet

Moderate

Deer Run Trail

Deer Run Trail is located in O'Neil Woods, a unit of Metro Parks, Serving Summit County. You can reach O'Neil Woods by taking Riverview Road to Ira Rd. Turn west on Ira, then left onto Martin Road. The entrance to O'Neil Woods is less than a mile up Martin Road.

Deer Run Trail follows high ridges, drops down to Yellow Creek, then climbs back up a steep hillside to finish the 1.8 mile loop. Though relatively short, the climbs provide a good workout. Areas of mature upland oak forest, streamside sycamores and willows, fields of goldenrods, and an alder swamp are all found along this trail. The diversity of habitat makes it a favorite trail for birders.

Begin Deer Run Trail at the eastern edge of the parking area, hiking the loop in a clockwise direction. Watch for the Metro Parks' "deer print" symbol signs. As you begin the loop, you pass through old fields which are managed for bluebird habitat. These fields are also favored habitat for woodcocks, or "timberdoodles" which perform their mating rituals here in the spring. Entering an oak woods, you will find a bench strategically placed at the trail summit overlooking a steep drop. There are fine views of the valley here while descending 69 steps along the ridge. Another 76 steps and switchbacks take you to the valley below, a total descent of 180 feet.

Cross Bath Road and follow the trail towards Yellow Creek, a tributary of the Cuyahoga River. Here large sycamores, willows, cottonwoods and black walnuts line the path along the stream. You can also find ferns, wildflowers, the rope-like bittersweet vines, and virgin's bower vines. Several wood bridges take the trail across side creeks. Leaving the creek, Deer Run Trail passes through a field and along an alder swamp, one of the few in Summit County.

The trail crosses a side creek on stepping stones, then again crosses Bath Road and begins the ascent back to the picnic area. You will climb about 150' in a third of a mile. It gets your heart pumping! Again, benches along the way provide some welcome rest and views of the wooded ravines. The trail emerges from the woods at the top of the ridge into the picnic area near where you began.

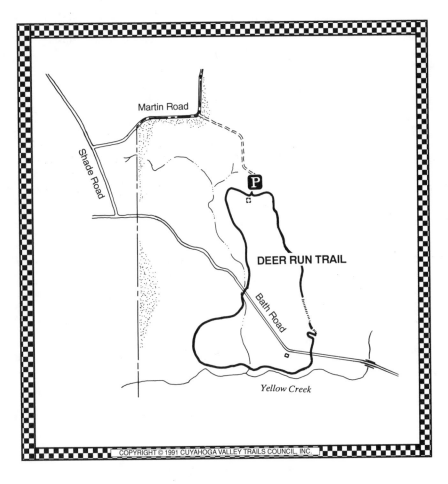

Deer Run Trail

The information on trails given here is accurate and up-to-date as of the summer of 1991. As the trail system within Cuyahoga Valley National Recreation Area is still developing, the intention is to revise this volume every few years. If you have comments or suggestions, please forward to: Cuyahoga Valley Trails Council, Inc., 1607 Delia Ave., Akron, OH 44320-1617.

APPENDIX

For More Information write or call:

Superintendent
Cuyahoga Valley National Recreation Area
15610 Vaughn Road
Brecksville, OH 44141
216-526-5256 or 216-650-4414

Cleveland Metroparks
4101 Fulton Parkway
Cleveland, OH 44144
216-351-6300

Metro Parks, Serving Summit County
975 Treaty Line Road
Akron, OH 44313
216-867-5511

Reservable Picnic Shelters

There are several reservable picnic areas throughout CVNRA. A fee is charged for use of these areas. All offer a covered picnic shelter and room for a large group. Each is surrounded by a large outdoor play area and access to hiking trails. All have grills for cooking and restrooms.

Following is a list of these areas and telephone numbers to contact for reservations.

Cleveland Metroparks (216-351-6300)

       Brecksville Reservation:
       Ottawa Point

       Bedford Reservation:
       Lost Meadows (reservable on weekends only)

Reservations are taken starting January 2 for the current year.

Metro Parks, Serving Summit County (216-867-5511)
    Furnace Run:
    Brushwood Shelter   (reservable six months in advance; enclosed and
    includes kitchen with refrigerator and coffee maker; wood burning fire-
    place)

Cuyahoga Valley National Recreation Area (216-650-4636)

    Kendall Ledges Shelter
    Octagon Shelter

Reservations are open on January 2 and must be made at least four weeks in
advance. Fee is half price for persons with Golden Age Passports or Golden Access
cards.

Overnight Lodging Within CVNRA

The Inn at Brandywine Falls
George and Katie Hoy, Innkeepers
8230 Brandywine Road
Sagamore Hills, OH 44067
216-467-1812 or 650-4965
Call for reservations

Northeast Ohio Council of AYH
Stanford House AYH Hostel
6093 Stanford Road
Peninsula, OH 44264
216-467-8711
Reservations advised for weekends; any age welcome;
not necessary to be AYH member

Dover Lake Park
P.O. Box 192
Northfield, OH 44067
216-467-SWIM or 216-650-FLOW
Tent and trailer camping year-round
Water park open during summer

Further Reading

The following books were used as references and may be of interest to those wanting to learn more about the Cuyahoga Valley. Most are available at CVNRA visitor centers or in the CVNRA library.

Ellis, William Donohue. *The Cuyahoga*. Dayton, Ohio: Landfall Press, 1966.

Gieck, Jack. *A Photo Album of Ohio's Canal Era, 1825-1913*. Kent, Ohio: Kent State University Press, 1988.

Horton, John J. *The Jonathan Hale Farm*. Cleveland, OH: The Western Reserve Historical Society, 1961.

Jackson, James S. and Margot. *The Colorful Era of The Ohio Canal*. Peninsula, OH: Cuyahoga Valley Association, revised edition, 1988.

_____. *Cuyahoga Valley Tales*. Peninsula, OH: Cuyahoga Valley Association, 1985.

Jesensky, Joseph D. *Pages From a Tinkers Creek Valley Sketch Book . . 1923-1933*. Northampton Historical Society, 1980; reprinted by the Society 1987.

Lafferty, Michael B., Editor-in-Chief. *Ohio's Natural Heritage*. Columbus, OH: The Ohio Academy of Science, 1979.

Lupold, Harry F. and Haddad, Gladys, eds. *Ohio's Western Reserve*. Kent, OH: The Kent State University Press, 1988.

Manner, Barbara M. and Corbett, Robert G. *Environmental Atlas of the Cuyahoga Valley National Recreation Area*. Monroeville, PA: Surprise Valley Publications, 1990.

Palmer, E. Laurence. *Fieldbook of Natural History*. Second edition, Revised by H. Seymour Fowler. New York: McGraw-Hill Book Company, 1975.

Peattie, Donald Culross. *A Natural History of Trees*. Second Edition. Boston: Houghton Mifflin Company, 1963.

Stokes, Donald W. *A Guide to Nature in Winter*. Boston: Little, Brown and Company, 1976.

Sifritt, Susan K. *A Field Guide to the Geology of the Cuyahoga Valley National Recreation Area*. Cleveland, OH: By the Author, 1983.